$\mathcal{B}razil$

Can no longer be used for credit
in the Reading Program.

1998 - Education for Mission
      (formerly Christian Global
      Concerns)

Brazil

A Gracious People in a Heartless System

Zwinglio M. Dias
and Joyce Hill

Friendship Press • New York

Copyright © 1997 by Friendship Press

Editorial Offices:
475 Riverside Drive, New York, NY 10115
Distribution Office:
P.O. Box 37844, Cincinnati, OH 45222-0844

Manufactured in the United States of America

Library of Congress Cataloging-in-Publication Data

Dias, Zwinglio M.
    Brazil : a gracious people in a heartless system / by Zwinglio M.
Dias and Joyce Hill.
    p. cm.
    Includes bibliographical references.
    ISBN 0-377-00315-8
    1. Brazil – Church history. 2. Church and social problems – Brazil.
I. Hill, Joyce. II. Title.
BR675.D53 1997
278.1–dc21   96-40060
                                                 CIP

For Elizandra
for her love, affection, and patience
and Ernesto,
who lived and shared joy, hope,
and grace with me and
all who knew him

Contents

Chapter 6
The North American Response **81**

Preface

*T*HIS BOOK is intended to be a brief introduction for our sisters and brothers in the churches in North America to the people and churches of Brazil. It has been written by two Protestants, one from Brazil and one from the United States, working in mission.

Although we are moving beyond the old model of mother (donor) churches and daughter (recipient) churches, because of our history, some forms of dependency of the South on the North may remain. We need to understand that the future of the evangelical faithfulness of our churches in both hemispheres depends on our ability to accept and share different historical views, to learn from each other, and to stand together in solidarity in the face of the daily struggles and sufferings that beset us. Brazil and its churches have much to say to our brothers and sisters in the North, who in turn must dispel the image of a missionary effort that was often arrogant and triumphalistic. The authors will be more than satisfied if readers feel touched by the history that we narrate and by the challenges that God, the Lord of history, offers us through history.

Acknowledgments

ZWINGLIO DIAS wishes to express his appreciation to his colleague Lais Menezes, to whom he owes much of the economic analysis in chapter 3. He also wishes to thank Friendship Press for offering KOINONIA: Ecumenical Presence and Service the privilege of addressing our sisters and brothers of the churches in North America.

Joyce Hill acknowledges with thanks the contribution of Wilma Roberts of the General Board of Global Ministries of the United Methodist Church to the stories of mission, notably the account of the Potiguara Indians. She also expresses gratitude to the Latin American Council of Churches for permission to translate and print the poems of the late Ernesto Barros Cardoso and of Napoleão Marcos Mendes. She is grateful to Simei Monteiro and the Methodist Church in Brazil for permission to translate and print their poems.

The editors note that they found Joseph Page's *The Brazilians* (1995) particularly helpful in preparing this resource and recommend it to those who would like to read further on the subject.

The drawings heading each chapter were executed by Paul Lansdale. They are adapted from Brazilian artifacts.

Chapter 1.   Wrought iron from a colonial doorway in
              Salvador
Chapter 2.   Motif from the base of a Carnival float
Chapter 3.   Carved wooden window shutter in Rio
Chapter 4.   Wings of a paper kite
Chapter 5.   Necklace from a Carnival costume
Chapter 6.   Sidewalk mosaic from the beachside promenade
              in Rio

Introduction

*B*RAZIL is one of the foremost countries in the world. It ranks fifth in land area (more than 3 million square miles) and sixth in population (more than 160 million people). Its warm climate, abundant resources, and thriving industry put its economy in eighth place in 1989. Yet despite these material advantages, which could provide a comfortable living for its people, Brazil has been exploited throughout its history. Foreign countries and corporations have exploited its riches to their own advantage, and the Brazilian upper classes have exploited their own people. In 1989, 10 percent of the population owned more than 50 percent of the national income and more than 80 percent of the land. At the other end of the scale, 25 percent of the population suffered from chronic malnutrition. About 66 percent were poor, many of them unemployed. Brazil's per capita income is next to the lowest in the world. The gulf between rich and poor, which exists in most countries, is perhaps greater in Brazil than anywhere else in the world.

On a spiritual level, Brazil was colonized under the sign of the cross, and it has the largest Roman Catholic population of any country. Yet it never became a Catholic nation. Many who call themselves Catholic are only nominal believers. Many have mixed their faith with elements of Indian and African religions. Catholics became bitter rivals of late-arriving Protestant missions, which, despite heroic efforts, have failed to develop a thriving Brazilian Protestantism. Thus Brazil continues to be a "mission field" because the Christ proclaimed by Catholics and Protestants was different from the one in the gospel. The "missionary process"

1

really represented the interests of the Portuguese on the one hand and the United States on the other. Mission in the true sense is to live with and for others to create an abundant life for all, using the contributions that each person can bring. But both Catholic and Protestant missions (except for some Pentecostals) tried to impose their own Latin or Anglo-Saxon version of the gospel. They generally ignored or disdained anything that Indians, blacks, or mulattos had to offer and considered them to be objects of mission rather than accepting them as sisters and brothers.

Brazil, the United States, and Canada share many historical similarities. All three began as European colonies motivated by both religious fervor and the desire for economic gain. All three were forged by European immigrants who steadily marched west, conquering vast territories, destroying the native peoples and cultures, and exploiting the land. Brazil and the United States introduced labor-intensive agriculture requiring slaves. All three took European models as their standard for many years. All three have a history of violence. All three are part of the world capitalist system with its ever increasing tension between rich and poor. But Brazil was quite different from Anglo North America in its dominant religion, its form of colonial government, and its attitudes toward government, the individual, and the work ethic. Moreover, it was a latecomer to capitalism, industrialization, and democracy. Consequently, as it developed it went to greater extremes than the North with quite different results.

The following three chapters will look at the history of Brazil and the shaping of Brazilian culture in an effort to understand its present social and economic problems. The next two chapters will describe the Christian presence in Brazil, its relation to other faiths of Brazilians, and what the churches are doing to respond to the people's needs. The final chapter considers what response North American Christians might make.

Chapter 1

The Formation of a Country

Brazil has never existed for itself in the sense of satisfying the needs of its own people for survival and prosperity. We have existed to meet the needs of others. Brazil is, and always has been, a mill for using people as grist. We have built ourselves up by burning millions of Indians. Later we burned millions of blacks. Now we are burning millions of mestizos in their production of things to bring profits to the business sector, not of things they themselves consume.

— D. Ribeiro, *O Brasil como problema*

*B*RAZIL'S five hundred years of history have brought it from a Portuguese colony to an independent nation among the ten richest in the world, but its journey has not benefited the great majority of its people.

Brazil is the largest country in South America, but neither its wealth nor its population are evenly distributed. The northern part of the country tends to be agricultural and poor, the southern part to have more industry and more money. Only 7 percent of the land is arable. The bulk of the population crowds into cities along the east coast. Most people would live in cities if they could. Mountains, tropical rain forest, and unnavigable rivers were obstacles to large-scale migration west until the introduction of roads and airlines in the late twentieth century.

The country may be divided into five geographic areas. The Northeast consists of a narrow fertile coastal strip, which historically supported large sugar and cacao estates, and the interior backlands (*sertão*), a dry pastureland subject to frequent drought. Many of its poor herders and subsistence farmers have migrated to other parts of Brazil. The Southeast is a highland region of gold and iron mines and of large agricultural estates and cattle ranches. The South is an area of large coffee estates, cattle ranches, small mixed farms, and industry. The Far West is a heavily forested frontier region presently undergoing development. In the northwest lies Amazonia, a huge area (42 percent of Brazil) of tropical rain forest occupying the valley of the Amazon and its tributaries. It too is now open to settlement and development.

Colony

In the late fifteenth century, venturesome Italian, Spanish, and Portuguese navigators were landing on the shores of South America, the Caribbean islands, and Africa in search of riches. To avoid conflict, in 1493, Pope Alexander VI drew a line through the Atlantic Ocean giving Africa and India to Portugal and South America to Spain. The Treaty of Tordesillas (1494) extended the papal line west to include eastern Brazil in Portugal's territory.

In 1500 the Portuguese navigator Pedro Alvarez Cabral, blown off course on his way to India, landed on the coast of Brazil. Although he planted a cross and claimed the land for Portugal, the Portuguese were more interested in the East. Even when their fortunes in India declined and they turned to Brazil, they had no intention of creating a nation in the New World. They regarded Brazil as a source of riches to be used to pay off the pressing debts of the Portuguese crown. They exploited their colony through a sequence of three resources: brazilwood, sugar, and gold.

Economic Growth and Exploitation

At first the crown allowed a few Portuguese merchants to harvest brazilwood (*caesalpina brasiliensis*), which was valued in Europe for the production of dyes for textiles. The French, who also wanted brazilwood, arrived, so the Portuguese crown decided to occupy the land. The crown divided it into fifteen huge captaincies, running inland from the coast, granted to nobles or other servants of the crown. They in turn gave large estates to their family and friends, who began to raise sugarcane, tobacco, and cotton along the Northeast coast and cattle in the Northeast backlands. Sugar, exported to Europe, was the leading crop in the seventeenth century.

Since there were few Portuguese colonists and they considered themselves gentlemen who did not work with their hands, labor was needed for the sugar plantations. The indigenous peoples, miscalled Indians, were unsuited to regular field work. They died, were killed by the Portuguese, or escaped into the forests of the interior. So the Portuguese, who were already using African slaves in Portugal, began to import them into Brazil in 1538. There they became, according to one historian, "the hands and feet of the sugar mill," maintained by "beatings, bread, and blankets."

Because most of the captains proved to be poor administrators, in 1549 the crown sent over a governor-general, who ruled with his court from his capital at Bahia (modern Salvador). He gave incentives to the sugar planters and drove the French out of Guanabara Bay, where Rio de Janeiro was founded in 1567. Meanwhile the crown was encouraging immigration. Thousands of Portuguese of all classes arrived. In 1654 local militia, including Indians and blacks, drove out Dutch planters who had settled in the Northeast in what is now the state of Pernambuco.

By the end of the century, Brazilian sugar had lost its monopoly as Dutch and French sugar plantations developed in the Caribbean, and the Northeast began to decline. But the Portuguese were already venturing into the Amazon Valley, to forestall the French, and into other parts of the interior in search of new pastureland and Indians to enslave. In the 1690s groups of armed adventurers called *bandeirantes* discovered gold in the Southeastern Highlands in what is now the state of Minas Gerais.

The discovery set off a gold rush as Portuguese colonists, slaves, and new immigrants hurried to establish mining camps, where they fought with the *bandeirantes* and sometimes ran out of food. Ouro Preto became a major center. In 1763 the capital was moved south to Rio.

Most of the work was done by black slaves. Most of the gold went out of the country either to pay the crown tax of 20 percent or to buy luxurious imports from Europe for the mine owners. It has been said that in one way or another it was the gold dug from the bowels of Brazil that helped finance the Industrial Revolution.

Stirrings Toward Independence

Brazil was too big for Portuguese law, administered now by a viceroy and often corrupt, incompetent, or easygoing officials, to be effective. Moreover, Brazilians were restive under Portuguese taxes on imports and restrictions on the colony's right to trade with other countries or to develop domestic industries, the policies of the mercantile system. Inspired by the American Revolution, which represented Americans' similar dissatisfaction with Britain, and the French Revolution, Brazilians started several small, secret independence movements. The most important was the rebellion in which

Brazilians of Portuguese descent in Minas Gerais took up arms against Portuguese loyalists in 1789. Their leader was a dentist and militia officer known as Tiradentes ("Toothpuller"). The colonial authorities quickly subdued them and cut Tiradentes into four pieces for public display.

At the beginning of the nineteenth century, Europe was engulfed by the Napoleonic Wars. Portugal allied itself with Britain against France, which invaded Spain and Portugal in 1807. Fleeing the French, the Portuguese regent, Dom João, took his entire court into exile in Brazil. In 1808 they arrived in Rio, which now became the capital of the Portuguese Empire. To upgrade his provincial new capital, Dom João established a university and library; started a printing press, a bank, and a mint; and opened Brazil to world trade — all previously forbidden to the colony. He created a bureaucracy headed by Portuguese exiles but including Brazilians. In 1816, when his mother, the mad queen, died, Dom João took the title of João VI of Portugal and Brazil, thus elevating Brazil to the rank of kingdom.

When Dom João was recalled to Portugal in 1821, he left his son, Dom Pedro, as regent. In 1822, when the Portuguese assembly tried to reduce Brazil to colonial status and ordered the prince home, he refused to go, declaring, "Independence or die." Shortly after, he was crowned emperor. The Portuguese troops withdrew with little violence, but Portugal insisted that Brazil assume Portugal's debt to Britain. So Brazil was born with a ready-made foreign debt.

Empire

As emperor, Pedro I ruled under the Constitution of 1824, which gave him broad powers and made for continued conflict with the newly elected legislative assembly of large landowners and businessmen. He was also torn between his loyalty to his new country and his loyalty to Portugal, where his father died in 1820. Unable to resolve these tensions, he abdicated and sailed for Portugal in 1831, leaving his five-year-old son, Pedro, as regent. After a decade of local rebellions, the handsome, amiable, scholarly fourteen-year-old prince was crowned emperor in 1840.

During the peaceful, prosperous reign of Pedro II, Brazil's economy developed more rapidly. The gold supply was depleted as a result of intense pressure to export more to Europe, but coffee and cattle, raised on huge estates in the Southeast and the South, became major exports. A British company began to build railroads in these regions. Steamships were built. New factories produced food, textiles, and goods for export, and São Paulo and eastern and southern cities flourished.

Although the Brazilian economy was no longer under the control of Portugal, it now became a satellite of British interests. Britain, at the forefront of the Industrial Revolution in Europe, wanted food and raw materials for its cities and factories and markets for its manufactured goods. In this new industrial economy, slavery was no longer a cost-effective means of production. Britain abolished slavery in its own territories in 1833 and put pressure on Brazil to do likewise. After decades of internal political struggle, Brazil finally ended slavery in 1888, the last country in the Western world to do so.

The immediate consequences were disastrous. The state had made no provisions to recompense the great landowners, who had lost the labor force that made their estates profitable. Neither had the state given the former slaves any land, tools, or training with which to make a living. Their former owners hired some back at wretchedly low pay, but they had no more interest in their well-being because they were no longer property. Overnight the blacks were transformed into an army of unemployed.

The disgruntled landowners withdrew their support from the emperor. Restive army officers who had fought in the War of the Triple Alliance (1865–1870) with Uruguay and Argentina that nearly destroyed Paraguay, were also disillusioned with the empire. These groups joined forces to overthrow Pedro II in 1889 and declare a republic.

Republic

As a republic, Brazil lurched along successively controlled by landowners, a dictator, industrialists, and the military. Economic policy was nearly always in their favor, seldom concerned with the welfare of the masses of the people.

Old Republic

The Constitution of 1891 authorized a government controlled by the great landowners of the Southeast and the South, notably the states of São Paulo, center of coffee production, and Minas Gerais, center of the dairy industry. They established the so-called Coffee and Milk Policy and agreed that representatives of each state (*paulistas* and *mineiros*) would take turns holding the presidency and the power. They ensured that the government subsidized the coffee growers, encouraged exports, and kept wages low.

The imperial government had already encouraged European immigrants to settle in the South to offset pressures from former Spanish colonies that had become the independent countries of Uruguay and Argentina. The republican government redoubled efforts to attract European and other immigrants, offering free ocean passage, land, and subsidies. It was believed that Europeans would make more intelligent, efficient workers in the expanding coffee industry and other businesses than the uneducated black former slaves. Several million immigrants arrived between 1820 and 1930 — Portuguese, Spanish, German, Italian, Eastern European, Middle Eastern, and Japanese.

Some went to the Amazon Valley, which was experiencing a boom in rubber. Many more settled in the Southeast and South, which were cooler and more fertile. Eventually many of them bought their own small, prosperous farms, raising both crops and animals. Others became successful businessmen. especially in the textile and food industries. Such people, along with lesser officials in the large government bureaucracy and army officers, formed a small middle class.

A disputed election in 1929 involving accusations of fraud and an assassination led to the Revolution of 1930. Dissatisfied politicians and the military overthrew the *paulista* president and installed Getúlio Vargas, a politician from Rio Grande do Sol, in the far south, as provisional head of state.

The Vargas Years and the Aftermath

Vargas controlled Brazil for fifteen years, putting down a *paulista* rebellion in 1932, issuing the Constitution of 1934, and becoming dictator by a coup d'état in 1937. He supported the coffee growers, who were suffering from a fall in prices as a result of the Great Depression of 1929, but he also favored cotton growing and stock raising as diversification.

Influenced by the Nazi and Fascist movements that exalted nationalism in Germany and Italy, Vargas began to build a nationalist program in Brazil to modernize the country, increase the people's pride in it, and free it of its economic ties to Britain. To these ends he used government funds to build railroads, shipping, and heavy industry, earning the title "mother of companies." Seeking aid for his program in the United States, he sent Brazilian troops to Europe in World War II to fight on the side of the United States and its Allies. In return, the United States gave Brazil the first large steel mill in Latin America.

Through tariffs on imported goods, government loans, tax credits, and price-and-wage controls, Vargas encouraged Brazilian industry for the domestic market, although often the goods were inferior. These measures also ensured that industry would be dependent on the state. Similarly, he created the Ministry of Labor, which had the sole authority to recognize labor unions and supervise their officers and funds. This measure and a minimum wage law seemed to favor workers — Vargas was called the father of the poor in the media — but actually put them in the power of the state.

After the war, Brazil returned to formal democracy and issued the Constitution of 1946, which still prevented the illiterate majority from voting. Industrialization slowed, inflation rose, workers struck, and Vargas was elected president in 1950 with tremendous popular support. Unable to solve the economic problems or overcome conservative opposition, he committed suicide in 1954.

Vargas's death was not in vain. It impeded the more conservative groups, who favored rich Brazilians and foreign businesses, most of them in the United States, from taking power. Under President Joscelino Kubitschek (1956–1960) the pace of industrialization picked up. The government sponsored many large-scale projects such as the building of Brasília, in the interior, which became the new capital in 1960. To pay for these projects, the government printed more money than was backed by goods and services. In six years (1955 to 1961) cruzeiros in circulation rose from 60 billion to about 200 billion. Some people made fortunes, but the resulting inflation was especially hard on the poor.

Conflict between the Left, which wanted higher wages, land reform, or even a Marxist revolution, and the conservative Right, combined with continued inflation, created political unrest. Foreign businesses and banks no longer wanted to invest in Brazil. In 1964 the military staged a coup, with United States' approval, and seized the government from the somewhat leftist president, João Goulart.

Military Dictatorship

Brazil's military rulers, with advisers from the United States, made strikes illegal, subdued the unions, capped salaries, ended workers' tenure rights, and produced the Constitution of 1967. Using two workers' strikes and student demonstrations as an excuse, in 1968 they began a policy of merciless repression, imposing censorship, removing suspected subversives from union and faculty posts, restricting political rights, and crushing guerrilla risings. Newly established welfare benefits were dismantled. Thousands of Brazilians were forced into exile. Hundreds died of torture at the hands of the military.

This repression cleared the ground for the Brazilian "Miracle," a period of astounding economic growth. The government financed or helped finance factories for automobiles and other heavy goods, roads into the interior, oil wells, mines, airlines, and hydroelectric plants. A great deal of the necessary capital was borrowed from international banks or foreign businesses because the inequitable tax system did not provide

National Congress
Building, Brasília
*Photo by Marcelo de
Oliveira/Imagens da Terra*

enough capital. Moreover, Brazilians who had money tended to spend it on living well or sent it abroad, safe from inflation and political upheavals, rather than put it in local banks or buy shares of stock in Brazilian companies. The use of foreign capital meant that the government had to pay interest and give benefits to its creditors rather than use the money for social services for its own people. It also meant that capital was spent on projects that would reap great profits for the owners rather than meet the basic needs of the people.

When world oil prices rose in 1973 and 1974, Brazil, like many developing countries that depended on imported oil, had to borrow even more money. The greater its debt, the more money it printed, which increased inflation still more, at one point reaching 2000 percent in a year.

During all this economic turmoil, landholding remained the same as in colonial days, largely in the hands of great landowners. The introduction of mechanized agriculture and the conversion of farmland into factories meant that far fewer tenant farmers and sharecroppers were needed. The excess workers began to occupy large unproductive private estates or migrated to cities in search of work. At the same time, the population increased far beyond the available jobs.

The military government, unable to solve these problems and under criticism from labor unions and the Roman Catholic Church, little by little gave up its powers. In 1985 it returned the state to the rule of constitutional law.

Democracy Restored

The Constitution of 1988 reduced the power of the president and increased the electorate to all Brazilians over sixteen, including the illiterate. But it made little change in Brazil's economic woes. New, more progressive political parties emerged, notably the Workers' Party, led by Luís Inácio "Lula" da Silva, which tried to propose an economic policy more favorable to the common people than the competition in the capitalist world economy pursued by the state. Lula ran a close second to Fernando Collor de Mello, who was elected president in 1989, promising to end corruption. Three years into his presidency, however, because of scandals and corruption, Collor himself was impeached in 1992 — the first presidential impeachment in Brazilian history. He peacefully resigned. By 1993, Brazil had dropped from eighth place in the world economy in 1988 to fourteenth.

In 1993 President Itamar Franco made the former professor of sociology and the senator of the republic, Fernando Henrique Cardoso, minister of the economy. Cardoso created an economic plan that authorized a new currency pegged to the dollar, privatized government-owned businesses, welcomed foreign imports, and continued to renegotiate the foreign debt. Inflation dropped, agreement on the debt was reached, and Cardoso also defeated Lula at the polls. Regarding his presidency, some Brazilians were optimistic; others doubted the likelihood of fundamental reforms.

Chapter 2

The Formation of a People

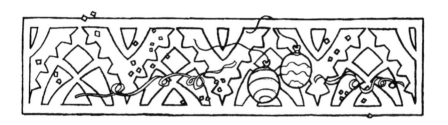

SONGS TO SING

We have songs to sing,
Strength we have to sing,
As we plant the seeds
That the flowers will bring,
Strengthen those in pain,
Sharing their concern.
We believe that springtime
Always will return.

Watching the people who laugh and dance
Later to struggle for life itself,
We know that hope is reborn
We know that life is reborn.

— Simei Monteiro,
translated by Joyce Hill

*I*N A COUNTRY that merges three peoples, each with its own distinct cultural traditions, can we speak of a Brazilian people with an authentically Brazilian culture? Have Brazilians developed a way of living in the world that is different from the way developed in Western Europe and North America? To answer these questions, let us look more closely at the three groups that make up modern Brazilians: the dominant Portuguese and other European immigrants, the indigenous peoples (Indians) who have managed to survive, and the Africans, the most vigorous of all.

Europeans and Other Immigrants

Most of the millions of Portuguese who arrived in Brazil from the sixteenth to the twentieth century came to make their fortune, or at least their living. Except for the Jesuits, Franciscans, and secular clergy who came to win converts and strengthen the faithful, most were in search of opportunity beyond that offered in their small, poorly endowed homeland. Unlike the English colonists in North America, most Portuguese colonists of the period hoped to return home to spend their New World riches. Only later did they plan to settle permanently.

Meanwhile, as was true of many Europeans in the New World, they regarded the land as something to be conquered and used, not respected and protected. Disdaining the indignity of manual labor, in the Portuguese aristocratic tradition, they pressed first the Indians and then African slaves to clear the land and work their plantations, ranches, and mines.

The Portuguese and their Brazil-born descendants, the Creoles, did not hesitate to use these dark-skinned non-Europeans as tools for the Portuguese advantage or destroy them. Since there were few Portuguese women in the early days, Portuguese and Creole men often lived with Indian women. Later, in the eighteenth century, the government encouraged intermarriage between whites and Indians in order to integrate the Indians into the Portuguese Brazilian population. Their offspring, however, the *caboclos,* tended to occupy the bottom ranks of society.

Many Portuguese and Creole men, even if married to white women, had children by black slave women. These racially mixed offspring, mulattos, were often recognized by their fathers and freed or even allowed to inherit property. But many, like the *caboclos,* were looked down on as nobodies. Generally having a dark skin was a disadvantage.

Along with these negative attitudes toward land, work, and nonwhites, the Portuguese brought their language, their literary tradition, a sturdy practical sense, the ability to adapt to circumstances, and a strong patriarchal family system that protected and demeaned women. Their religious sense could be fatalistic or devotional but was more easygoing than that of Spain. Finally, until the twentieth century, the Portuguese held the conviction that European culture was superior to anything Brazil produced.

Later, immigrants from other countries brought their own traditions. Hardworking Germans maintained their own language, schools, and Lutheran faith in the small communities that grew up around their prosperous farms in the South. Some of them did well in breweries, shoes, and textiles; they founded Varig Airlines and a worldwide jewelry business. During World Wars I and II, in which Brazil with other powers fought against Germany, they were pressed to enter into the Brazilian mainstream.

Italians, who included socialists, and Eastern Europeans did well in farming and business. Many Arabs from Lebanon and Syria became shopkeepers. They brought with them their Muslim faith. After the Civil War in the United States, defeated Southerners arrived, hoping to continue farming with slave labor. Protestant missionaries accompanied them. Japanese contract workers arrived in 1908 and thereafter to do farm labor in the South. Although many were exploited, they did well in vegetable farming, many becoming farm owners and businessmen. Like the Germans, they had their own schools, language, and newspapers. After World War II they attended Brazilian schools, lived in Brazilian cities, and began to marry Brazilians.

Indians

Perhaps 500,000 to 2 million Indians were living in Brazil when the Portuguese arrived. The Indians formed five language families and hundreds of nomadic tribes. The men were hunters and gatherers; the women raised manioc, maize, beans, and yams on plots burned from the forest and then allowed to return to forest to recover their fertility. Their religions were animistic, respectful of animals and land; they devoted a lot of time to tribal wars, some tribes ritually eating their victims.

The Portuguese regarded these primitive people as savages to be pacified, civilized, Christianized, and made to settle down and work for the colonists. Although the Jesuits tried to protect them, the landowners and *bandeirantes* generally won out. But Indian men scorned farm work as fit only for women. Many died in the fields or in wars stirred up by the Portuguese or from European diseases such as smallpox and measles. Others fled inland. The women, used by the Portuguese men, produced the half-breed *caboclos,* who often worked as scouts or on ranches in the backlands.

Later, when Brazilians were making fortunes in rubber, they enslaved the Indians of the Amazon to tap rubber trees. Many died in battles with migrant rubber tappers from the Northeast *sertão.*

Thanks to the influence of an army officer of Indian extraction, Cândido Mariano da Silva Rondon, the government established the Service for the Protection of Indians (SPI) in 1910. It was supposed to preserve the Indians and their tribal cultures, but as ranchers and other settlers from the South streamed west and made deals with corrupt officials, little was done. Many Indians were killed and their land seized for development. When Brazil's military government discovered these misdeeds, they created a new National Indian Foundation (FUNAI) in 1967, but it, too, is under constant pressure from land-hungry settlers and developers, rendering the laws ineffectual. Even though Indians can now vote, since the Constitution of 1988 ended the literacy requirement, they are too few (about 200,000) and scattered to have much power.

The Indian legacy is some vocabulary, canoes and hammocks, and foods such as manioc and maize. The Indians also bequeathed their descendants a love of rhythmic music and colorful dress, belief in animal spirits and faith healing, dislike of restrictions, and a taste for cleanliness and wandering.

Blacks

People of African descent make up the largest part of Brazil's mestizo (mixed) population. They range in color from black to shades of brown to white. Many people who consider themselves white have African blood. In the past, Brazilians of European descent tended to look down on black African slaves as diluting the population and contributing to Brazil's sense of inferiority in relation to Europe. Today many see blacks as an enriching element in the Brazilian mix.

Slavery, the treatment of one human being as the property of another, flourished in Africa long before it reached the New World. The Arabs, who were dominant in North Africa and the Middle East in the Middle Ages, bought and sold African slaves. When Spanish discoveries in the New World and new Portuguese trade routes to the East broke the Arab monopoly on world trade, Arab wealth and the Arab slave trade declined. Black African kingdoms in the Sudan region in northern Africa created their own slave trade, using black war victims captured from weaker tribes. They sold their captives to Portuguese and other European traders. The Portuguese began using slave labor in the islands of the

Azores and Madeira in the fifteenth century. They were quick
to bring slaves to their New World colony.

From 1583 to 1850, when the slave trade was made illegal,
perhaps 3 million to 4 million blacks survived the miserable
three-month sea passage to Brazil, many more than entered
the United States. According to one estimate, in 1825 there
were almost 2 million slaves in a total population of 4 million. Life expectancy for slaves was eighteen years, in contrast
to thirty-five for slaves in the United States.

The blacks brought to Brazil came principally from the
Atlantic coast of Africa. A large number belonged to the
Yoruba, Dahomey, and Fanti-Ashanti people in the Sudan region. Smaller numbers came from Gambia, Sierra Leone, the
Malagueta Coast, and the Ivory Coast. Another large number
belonged to the Mali and other groups in northern Nigeria,
who had an Islamic culture. Still others, the Bantu, came
from sub-Sahara Africa. Some blacks from the Sudan and
Nigeria had great pride in their sophisticated cultures and
kept their languages, stories, and beliefs, although they also
learned Portuguese and were baptized as Christians. Bantus
tended to adapt more readily to their new life.

All the blacks were put to work, at first in the sugar plantations of the Northeast, where they are still the largest part
of the population. Eventually they did all the fieldwork and
much mining all over Brazil. They also learned crafts and
worked in the house. Most white children were raised by
black nannies. All but the poorest Brazilians had at least one
slave. The availability of cheap black labor encouraged already indolent white Brazilians to assume there was no reason
for them to work at all.

Some slaves, especially house slaves, were well treated, and
they had many holidays. Slave families could not be broken
(unlike the situation in the United States), and they could
buy their freedom or win it by joining the army. But owners never forgot that blacks were there to work. Male slaves
were harshly treated and punished "for any misdeed, proven
or not, using tools of punishment that were not even used

on animals," according to the historian D. Ribeiro. Various slave risings, mostly by Sudanese, in the nineteenth century were ruthlessly crushed by landowners supported by the government. Women slaves were used by white men for their pleasure. There was a great deal of racial mixing, although many men failed to acknowledge their mulatto offspring.

When the government finally abolished slavery, not only did it fail to provide for its new citizens, it also ordered the burning of its documents related to the slave trade. That decision, the Golden Law, could be seen as an indication of the low esteem in which the government held blacks and its wish to blot out a shameful part of its history. It also meant that former slave owners could not claim compensation for loss of their property.

The freed slaves gradually found their way back into the economy, many as sharecroppers or very low-paid laborers on the landowners' estates. Others found lowly jobs in mines, factories, and cities. There were no laws discriminating against them, as there were at that time in the United States. Nevertheless, most blacks found themselves socially and economically where they had been all along, at the bottom of the barrel.

Used to depending on their owners, many blacks were not accustomed to acting on their own initiative. They could not obtain an education in the woefully inadequate public school system. Most employers, who were white, preferred whites for the better-paying jobs. This preference was intensified by the Brazilian tradition of giving jobs to a wide network of relatives, friends, and godchildren. Even if a black did the same job as a white person, the black was paid less. Clearly in Brazil it was an advantage to be white.

Most blacks generally accepted their lower status. Many, however, married lighter-skinned people if they could. There were no barriers to mulattos, who began to gain schooling and jobs. Unlike in the United States, where people of any African ancestry were counted black, in Brazil they can count themselves anything they like. A large proportion of mulattos and *caboclos* count themselves, and are accepted as, white. That avenue up the socioeconomic ladder helps explain why Brazil has not had the race riots and black power movements that have marked the United States since the 1960s.

Meanwhile, elements of African culture have permeated all ranks of Brazilian society. *Feijoada,* a stew of black beans, pork, rice, manioc, and spices, first made by slaves, is the national dish. The samba is the national dance, especially as the dominant music of Carnival. African gods, as discussed in chapter 4, have made their way into religious life.

The Brazilians

These strands of Portuguese, Indian, and African culture have been woven into the rich fabric of Brazilian life. The mulattos and *caboclos* especially, in their search for ethnic identity, gave form, color, rhythm, and flavor to being Brazilian.

Brazilians of all backgrounds share the Portuguese language, the Roman Catholic Church, a sense of optimism, and a genial courtesy. They joyously participate in Carnival, a week of parties, balls, and parades at the end of summer before the beginning of Lent. Rooted in ancient Greek and Roman festivals, adapted by the medieval church, Carnival in Brazil is a time of celebration, freedom, and escape from daily life into a world of fantasy. People in spectacular costumes (men dressed as women, poor as rich) dance and sing to the driving drum beat of samba bands. The costumes, songs, and themes of parade floats express Brazilian creativity, nationality, and social criticism, for example, of exploitation of the Amazon rain forest.

Brazilian national pride is also reflected in grandiose building schemes, such as the handsome modern architecture of Brasília and the vast highways and dams of the interior. Brazilians are especially proud of their soccer teams. The game, introduced by the British, began as an upper-class pastime but was enthusiastically adopted by the poor. Cheering, flag-waving crowds jam soccer stadiums in the cities, and most of the population follows the fortunes of professional Brazilian teams, which since the 1930s, have won many World Cups.

There are also disturbing strands in the Brazilian fabric. Brazilians may resort to violence to achieve their ends, as for example in their treatment of Indians, unruly slaves, political opponents, troublesome street children, and women who anger them. Their experiences with the Roman Catholic Church, slavery, an authoritarian government, and a savage economic system tend to make them fatalistic and dependent on others rather than reliant on their own efforts. These same experiences do not encourage a sense of individual worth in the self or others. There is often little respect for human life. Many Brazilians, however, feel that personal connections, the *compadre* system, are more important in life than objective merit or the rule of law. They are more inclined to rely on a network of favors given and received than on strict obedience to traffic lights, income tax laws, or job requirements. Their optimism, spontaneity, and ability to think big may defeat them when they do not take the pains to plan ahead and do not take into account the dimensions of the national and international economic structures that frustrate their efforts to realize their dreams.

— *Life in a* Favela —

Many of these facets of the Brazilian way of living can be seen in the life of Dom Antonio and his family. Dom Antonio, age fifty-eight, is a mulatto who lives in a *favela* (slum) on the outskirts of Rio. He was born in the Northeast *sertão,* where he was a small sharecropper. Almost thirty years ago, a severe drought ruined his harvest, he could not pay his rent, and he could not borrow money enough for seed for next season. The promised government help for the region never arrived. His landlord threw him off his plot of land. Dom Antonio and his wife, Dona Josefina, like millions in the *sertão*, made their way to the city in search of work.

Arriving in Rio without friends or money, Dom Antonio and Josefina settled in a tumbledown wood and cardboard shack crammed among others in a hillside *favela*. Pigs, chickens, dogs, and children, in ever increasing numbers, roamed the steep, dark alleys, which were flooded in the rainy season. There was no running water, electricity, sewage system, garbage collection, or fire or police protection, although just across the highway luxurious apartment houses and tennis courts lined Rio's famous beachfront.

Dom Antonio had never been to school, which only the rich could afford, and he had no other skills but farming. So he looked for work as a hod carrier on construction sites. Even though the wages were miserable, so many other men like Antonio were looking for work that finding a job, and keeping it, was a matter of luck. When Antonio was out of work, he sold candies and trinkets on the streets in the better parts of town. Josefina took in laundry, toting heavy cans of water from a distant spigot. Together they made barely enough to buy rice and beans to feed themselves and the four children that gradually arrived to fill their one room.

Today, Dom Antonio, like some of his neighbors on the lower slopes of the hill, has rebuilt his house with a concrete foundation and a metal roof. The city has piped in water, although it has not reached the squalid new shacks further up the hill built by the constant stream of newcomers. Antonio "borrows" electricity from a neighbor so that he can listen to his favorite soccer team on the radio. He enjoys a family Sunday dinner, cooked by Josefina, of chicken and spaghetti, oranges or bananas, and beer, in addition to the basic beans and rice.

Josefina still takes in laundry, but her elder son, Paulinho, delivers it to her customers when he is not flying kites with the other children on the top of the hill. Her elder daughter, Cristiane, travels by rickety bus two hours a day to work as a maid in a middle-class neighborhood. She gives some of her small wage to her mother but keeps some to pay her dues at one of Rio's fourteen samba schools. She rehearses the school's annual song and samba steps all year and sews an elaborate, yet revealing, costume to wear in the school's procession at Carnival. Josefina also takes part, as a *baiana,* one of a group of older women from Bahia, formerly samba dancers, who traditionally march in the procession whirling around in their old-style full skirts.

Woman Drawing
Water in a Rio
Favela
Photo by Richard Lord

Dom Antonio and Dona Josefina accept their hard life at the bottom of society with cheerful serenity and the hope that one day they can return home to their farm. They believe in their hearts that the Lord of all creation cares for them and their family with the help of many spirits who are in charge of specific aspects of creation. They go to church every Sunday, where they hear Mass and pray to Jesus and Mary, and as good Catholics, they try to do what Father Luís says. Ever since childhood, Antonio has learned that good relations with the church are important if you want to enjoy God's blessing.

Nevertheless, Antonio and Josefina have big problems, and Jesus and Mary may be too busy to listen to them, so they pray and light candles also to saints and guardian angels. They also believe there are other ways to reach God, especially through the *orixás* (pronounced oriSHA), powerful spirits that originated in Africa. Antonio and Josefina want to be on good terms with all the divinities who can be of help. Every Friday night Antonio goes to a *candomblé* temple to present an offering, usually food, and consult with its *orixá*. Josefina is an initiate in her *candomblé* temple, where she takes part in the ritual that calls on the *orixá* to take possession of the initiates. If one of her children is sick, because she cannot afford a doctor and there is no nearby public clinic, she may ask her *orixá* to drive the evil spirit out of the sick child. Cristiane sometimes goes to another temple to ask her *orixá* to help her find the right man. Antonio might also go to an Indian *pajetanza* ritual, which invokes the spirits of the rain forest to cast out sickness. Sometimes he goes to a Pentecostal service, where the minister exorcises the demon of sickness in the name of Christ. Antonio and Josefina know that Father Luís does not care much for this hodgepodge of belief, but neither does it matter to him if the people go to other places than his church for help.

Chapter 3

The "Miracle" and the Excluded

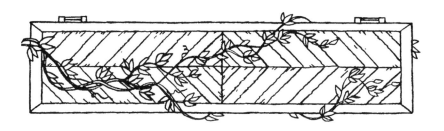

ON THE BANKS OF THE AMAZON

On the banks of the Amazon River
we sat down wept,
as we remembered our lands that were lost.
Today the invaders ask us to sing songs of joy
And those that deported us
order us to dance at their gates.
"Sing for us one of your songs,
Dance for us one of your dances."
How can we sing our songs in a strange land?
How can we dance at the gates of the oppressor?
Silence and weeping are our songs.
Our dance is a ritual of death,
they burned our homes
leaving them in ashes.
Our history lives within us!
We have opposed the conquerors

since the first day that the flood
of merchants covered our lands,
since they brought us "civilization"
and reduced our development to
messianic commercialism.
In a continent baptized
by the firing of cannons,
our religion called paganism,
faithfulness to our beliefs has been hidden
behind a mask to deceive the troops
who are exterminating us,
we children of the devastated Amazon.

Blessed are those who will dry up
the deep rivers formed by our tears!

— Napoleão Marcos Mendes,
translated by Joyce Hill

*B*RAZIL'S rapid economic development in the twentieth century blossomed into the "Miracle of Brazil." At the same time, it created an alarming gulf between the few rich and many poor who were pushed to the margin of Brazilian society or excluded from it entirely.

The "Miracle"

The explosive industrial growth of Brazil under the military dictatorship from 1969 to 1973 was an expression of the Western worldview shared by Europeans and Anglo North Americans. That view is based on the optimistic beliefs of the eighteenth-century Enlightenment that people can be educated to improve themselves and their circumstances and that such progress, aided by science and technology, is a good thing. Moreover, according to the nineteenth-century concept of evolution, human societies, like plants and animals, naturally evolve from a simple, "primitive" state to a more complex, advanced state that is "better" for all concerned.

As the Brazilian economist Lais Menezes points out, these
ideas formed at the same time that the capitalist system in
Europe was shaping the means of production. The process of
accumulating capital, the large amounts of goods or money
to invest in making more goods or money, was declared as
natural as eating or drinking. It was seen as an improve-
ment over earlier systems of production such as self-sufficient
farms or simple barter. Thus, progress, economic growth,
and capitalism were considered the same thing and the universal ideal. They continue to underlie the world capitalist
system today.

The countries that benefited most from this thinking were
its leading practitioners, Britain in the nineteenth century and
the United States after World War II. Fresh from its military
victory, the United States was the leader of the developed, industrialized, capitalist First World. The rest of the world was
seen as either Communist (the Second World) or backward
and underdeveloped (the Third World). President Harry S
Truman in his 1949 inaugural speech proclaimed that all the
peoples of the world should aim toward development. President John F. Kennedy, in the early 1960s, started the Alliance
for Progress, an ambitious program of economic aid to Latin
America, which sent much money to Brazil.

Because the attainment of a modern industrialized society
was considered so desirable, any means a government used
to achieve it were excused. Authoritarian governments ruling
by force rather than law, the trampling of civil liberties, government corruption, and even some economic suffering of
individuals, such as uprooted farmers, were excused or overlooked because nothing must be allowed to disturb the stable
society that was needed for economic growth. In the long
run, it was believed, such development would make up for
the sacrifices of human and social values.

Many Latin American political and economic leaders, especially in Brazil, adopted this optimistic capitalist philosophy.
In order to earn the capital needed to build the roads, railroads, hydroelectric plants, and factories needed to develop

the country, Brazil had to increase exports abroad and reduce costly imports by making industrial goods at home. The
government enthusiastically took the lead in carrying out this
policy. It gave tax credits and loans to great landowners to
modernize agriculture to increase production of cash crops
and to big businessmen to build heavy industrial plants to
make automobiles and machinery to sell at home and abroad.
It opened up the West to agriculture and industry. Many
of these new enterprises were owned and operated by the
government. Because exports and taxes were not bringing in
enough money, the government printed more money, which
caused prices to rise. It also borrowed capital from foreign
banks and the World Bank and encouraged U.S. and other
corporations to start businesses in Brazil. (See Table 1 in the
Appendix.)

The results of this relentless drive for economic growth
have not meant a better life for all Brazilians. A small group
of people made great fortunes, but life became harder and
harder for the rest of the population. The years of inflation pushed much of the middle class into the lower class
and most of the lower class into poverty. Brazil, like the
rest of the developing world, never realized the optimistic
capitalist dream.

The Excluded

Now it is too late. Brazil's "Miracle" is over and the military government is long gone, but life for the poor is getting
worse instead of better. In Brazil's agricultural past, the poor
could at least earn their food working in other people's fields.
As the country industrialized, landowners needed fewer field
hands, but new jobs opened up in construction and factories. The poor still sold their labor for pay. Since the 1980s,
however, new technologies such as computers are moving
the world's economic powers into a new, postindustrial age.
More and more workers in factories and offices are be-

ing displaced by machines. Companies and bureaucracies are downsizing. Millions of these superfluous workers are being let go. Without the resources to buy goods and services or to produce them to sell, they have no place in the world's market economy. In the new capitalist thinking, they are a dead weight that a healthy economy should get rid of as soon as possible. Brazil is perhaps not as far along this path as some countries, but it is headed in that direction. Its poor, already shoved to the margins of society, are being pushed over the edge.

The Rural Poor

In the past, Brazil's huge agricultural population worked on other people's land, but they felt secure on it and often had small plots for their own use. That changed. Some workers were no longer needed on large mechanized estates. Others, in the Northeast, could not survive a series of severe droughts. In both situations, tenants, sharecroppers, and day laborers had to leave the land, which continued to remain in the hands of large landowners as it had since colonial times.

Some of these displaced workers were promised land of their own or jobs in Rondônia and other parts of the newly opened North and West. But once they arrived, trucked over government roads, they found the land was already held by large landowners, it was infertile, or the government provided no seeds, food, or tools. Some of these landless poor squatted on undeveloped land, but they were forcibly ejected by the owners with government support. Others found themselves burning eucalyptus to make charcoal for factories, hopelessly in debt to their employers for transportation and food. Still others moved to the nearest city. At the same time, millions of displaced workers from the Northeast rode trucks or buses to coastal cities hoping to find factory jobs or other work and to enjoy the pleasures of city life. Gradually the huge countryside of Brazil was being emp-

Women and
Children Arriving
in the City
Photo by Richard Lord

tied as people flocked to nine metropolitan areas. Migration
to cities is going on all over the world, but it is particularly marked in Brazil. In 1991, 76 percent of the population
was urban.

The Urban Poor

For most of these new urban dwellers, the city is no answer either. There are not enough jobs for everyone, and they
often require education and skills that most of the poor do

not have. Because there is so much competition, wages are very low. Some people hold two or three jobs just to survive. Many have no official job at all. They sell candy, salvage from dumps, drugs, themselves.

To make matters worse, there is a great shortage of public services in the poorer slums where the penniless newcomers settle on vacant land that no one else wants because it is too steep or marshy or far from the center. Electricity, running water, sewerage and garbage disposal, telephones, public transportation and housing, and health clinics are inadequate or nonexistent. In some cities, 34 percent of garbage is piled up in open spaces, and 63 percent is dumped in rivers, creating a serious health hazard. In addition, there is air pollution from automobiles and factories; meanwhile, television displays all the tempting pleasures and luxuries that other Brazilians enjoy but the poor cannot afford.

Private enterprise sees no point in providing such services as electricity, telephone, and housing because the poor cannot pay for them. The military government had no money to spend on services either, or on providing welfare and unemployment checks because it was spending so much on heavy industry and servicing the debt. Although the subsequent democratic government has ended inflation and established a strong currency, it still has to pay the debt. In 1994, 62 percent of the federal budget was earmarked for interest and service charges, never mind principal.

Some slum dwellers, like Dom Antonio and Dona Josefina in chapter 2, have been able to maintain their faith and their family despite their harsh surroundings. Others have not been so lucky.

Street Children

Poverty and overcrowding have not reduced the population in Brazil, which continues to expand at an alarming rate. The annual increase in São Paulo in 1989 was 3.97, contrasted with 0.42 in New York. The population of Rio has doubled in the same time that the population of the Rio slums has increased ten times. Families of six or more children in one room, often with no father or an abusive stepfather and a mother with little or no income, find it difficult to stay together. For many, the solution is to send the older children, usually age seven to seventeen, into the streets. Some spend the day there and return home at night with any money they have come by. Others live full-time on the streets, sleeping in doorways or alleys or warehouses or over subway grates, alone or in gangs for protection. According to one report, 40 percent of Brazil's children, 25 million, are on the streets.

Although the Constitution of 1988 says that no children under fourteen shall work, most street children do, if they can find a job. Some work in hazardous shoe or glass factories. Others shine shoes, watch parked cars, sell candy or drugs, steal, or become prostitutes, both boys and girls. By law they cannot be punished, so the police round them up and put them in state-run correctional institutions. These are so underfunded and badly run that the children escape as soon as possible. Shopkeepers blame them for their poverty and consider them a menace to business. They approve or finance "death squads" of off-duty or retired police to clean up the streets. According to a Brazilian congressional report, four children are killed every day. One July night in 1993 in Rio, five boys who were sleeping in front of the Candelaria Cathedral were roused by six men and shot. The police were suspected. In 1989, 457 children were killed.

The government is not oblivious. The military dictatorship set up the National Foundation for the Well-Being of the Minor (FUNABEM), but it has not accomplished much. Later the Statute on Children and Adolescents provided for local councils to protect children's rights. It is not very effective. On the local level, the mayor of Curitíba has made a difference. Along with many city improvements, such as low-cost housing and a bus system, he set up forty centers to feed and teach street children. Private efforts to help street children, discussed in chapter 5, hardly scratch the surface.

— *Pedrinho Goes to Bed* —

The bedtime reflections of Pedrinho, who lives on the streets of Rio, give some insight into the plight of almost half of Brazil's children.

Pedrinho, an eight-year-old who looked twelve, had had a good day. He had not been beaten by the police, he had earned a few pennies watching a man's parked care, he had eaten a plate of warm beans and rice at a nearby church, and his favorite soccer team had won. The only thing missing was sharing a joint of marijuana with his friends, João and Carlinhos. Pulling his dirty, ragged blanket over him, he snuggled close to his two friends to escape the cold air of the autumn night. He wished it were summer again, but he was glad it was not raining, when he would have to seek cover in an abandoned warehouse.

Pedrinho had been living on the streets for three years. He seldom smiled, and his eyes had a hardened gleam. Sometimes he missed his mother and his eight brothers and sisters in the miserable shack in the *favela* of Catagalo on a hillside above the fashionable beachside district of Ipanema. But he was afraid of his mother's new man, whom he was supposed to call Daddy. "Daddy" spent his time gambling and drinking up what little money came his way. He seemed to enjoy hitting Pedrinho's tired mother for no good reason, and he often took a swipe at the children. Pedrinho had decided he was better off on his own.

Under his blanket, Pedrinho thought about the next day, which was all the future he could imagine. At dawn he would drag his newspapers and blanket to the garbage heap back of the bank, where they would be safe until the next night. He thought about how he could accumulate the fifteen cents he would need to pay his share of the money the street children collected each

Street Child
in Rio
*Photo by
Nando Neves/
Imagens da Terra*

week to pay the police to leave them alone. If they did
not pay, they would be arrested and sent to the government "home" for abandoned children, where innocent
boys met experienced young criminals, and everyone
was beaten for the slightest misbehavior. Pedrinho had
once run away from such a hell on earth; he never
wanted to see its doors again.

Pedrinho thought about his options. João and Car-
linho sometimes made money delivering drugs, but that
was risky because of the police. He could look for
salvage in a garbage dump. He could beg money from

drivers who stopped at a red light. He might try to sell hard candies that no one wanted. He might even steal a purse from a careless woman. He hoped he could get enough over the fifteen cents to buy a hamburger at McDonald's or at least some glue to sniff so that he wouldn't feel hungry. As he planned his future, he dropped off to sleep.

Women, Abuse, and Prostitution

Women and girls have seldom counted for much in Brazil's patriarchal society, which, as in most Latin American countries, was traditionally shaped for the convenience of men. Women were admired for their beauty or virtue, but they were kept firmly in second place. Marriages were arranged, and there was no divorce. Men were zealous in protecting their "honor" although not necessarily faithful to their wives. If such defense of honor meant violence toward another man or an erring wife, the incident seldom came to court, and if it did, the jury usually sympathized with the husband. Upper-class and middle-class women usually did not work outside the house as a matter of status. Lower-class women worked of necessity. Lacking education and economic independence, women had no choice but to accept their lot.

Despite this restrictive background, women have made strides in modern Brazil. Girls go to school and university, although there are not nearly enough public schools to take everyone. Working outside the house is no longer a loss of status, and many upper- and middle-class women do. In 1994 there were 38 women among the 305 members of Congress. The Constitution of 1988 allows divorce, forbids discrimination against women, and guarantees 120 days of maternity leave and protection from violence. Brazil's strong feminist movement led to a new concept, police stations run by and for women. Established in 1985, there are now 150.

Women police officers take cases of the abuse of women more seriously than men officers.

These gains, however, are of limited value. According to *U.S. News and World Report* (4 April 1994), white women earn half as much as men in similar jobs, and black women earn half as much as white women. The women's police stations are short staffed, and they can investigate only a tiny fraction of the complaints. Only 11 percent of women's cases ever reach court. If a man murders a woman, he usually spends just four years in jail. Because there are only three shelters for abused women in the whole country, women have little choice but to stay with violent men.

Violence against women in all classes continues, but the increased pressures of overcrowding and poverty have made it much worse among the poor. Lack of a job and other frustrations of not being able to live up to their macho society's expectations of men cause many men to abuse their women or abandon their families entirely. The mothers, needing money to support their children or the status that having a man brings, find other men to take the first one's place. These stepfathers often strike their stepchildren or sexually abuse the girls.

Poverty has also caused an increase in prostitution. Slum girls who are sexually abused at home and therefore disgraced or who are just hungry in a large family may escape to the street. There, without protection or money, they may be used by street boys or by paying customers or they may be put in brothels by madams or pimps. They are at the mercy of everyone, even the police.

— *Magali's "Madam"* —

Magali was a street child in São Bernardo, near São Paulo. She lived with several other children in a large cardboard packing crate. During the day she went to a class run by the National Ecumenical Street Children's

Ministry, where she learned to make candy to sell on the street. One night she did not return to the packing case. Anxious, the other children went to look for her. When they found that the police had picked her up at a street corner, they rushed off to get the only help they knew. Although it was late at night, they rang the doorbell of the home of Pastor Maria, who had befriended them.

When Pastor Maria opened the door, all the children piled in, all talking at once. As soon as she learned what the crisis was, she went off to the police station.

"I've come to get Magali."

"Oh, so you are her madam?" asked the police sergeant, assuming that was the only commanding adult a street girl would know.

"I am her pastor."

"Her pastor!" The sergeant was astounded. Pastor Maria stood her ground, and soon Magali was released in her care. Magali was lucky. She had not yet been beaten or sexually abused by the policeman on duty, as had happened to her friend Vande three weeks ago. She had a "family" of street children who sought help for her, and she had a pastor who risked being called a madam in order to rescue her.

— Two for the Price of One —

In Porto Velho, a town deep in Amazonia, the Reverend Luís had a sad experience. One day as he was showing a North American missionary woman through the local museum, two young girls approached her. Pointing to the pastor, one asked, "Is he your husband?'

"No," the missionary replied. "He is a friend."

"Is he a good friend?" the other girl asked?

"I am visiting the city for the day, and the pastor wanted me to see the museum" was the answer.

The girls thanked her and went across the room to talk to the pastor. Later he confessed to his visitor with some dismay, "They offered themselves to me, 'individually or together.' "

The two girls, eleven-year-old Claudia and twelve-year-old Marlene, had been recruited from the streets of São Paulo to "work" in a restaurant in this frontier Amazon town. Only after reaching there did they discover that the recruiter had been a pimp and their "work" was prostitution. Already in debt for the long bus trip and their food and lodging, a debt that increased every day, they could do nothing but submit. There was little chance of earning enough to pay off the debt and buy a bus ticket home. Claudia and Marlene are only two of thousands of girls from the streets of Brazil's cities who are lured north under false pretenses into a life of poverty and shame.

The Amazon Rain Forest and Its People

The vast Amazon Valley is a prime example of Brazilian economic exploitation and social violence. The region is home to nearly 4,000 plant and animal species and 150,000 Indians divided into 175 tribes. Its damp tropical heat, thick rain forest, and many diseases generally deterred Brazilian efforts to extract its riches. World demand for rubber in the late nineteenth century brought in Northeasterners, and Belém and other river towns prospered. Dutch East Indian rubber ended Brazil's rubber boom in 1912, and the area reverted to a hostile frontier.

The Brazilian "Miracle" brought change. The government wanted to develop the Amazon's timber, mineral, and water resources. It wanted to protect the region from invasions by Bolivia and from exploitation by the United States and other foreign countries. Finally, it wanted to attract displaced workers from the Northeast and South, proclaiming "Unpeopled Lands for Landless People."

To realize these aims, the government built roads to open up the interior. It gave tax credits to Brazilians and foreigners to buy land and invest in business. Rich Brazilian businessmen anxious to escape inflation bought vast stretches of rain forest to turn into pasture land. The U.S. businessman Daniel Ludwig bought 5,000 square miles in the Jari region in 1967 to harvest the timber and grow rice. The government directly owned and operated the huge mining complex at Carajás and the dams and hydroelectric plants at Tucuruí and Balbina.

Unfortunately, these grandiose schemes on paper did not work out as hoped. From an ecological point of view, they were a disaster. Miles of virgin forest fell to clear the land for ranches and the new industrial projects and roads. One estimate is that 5,800 square miles are lost each year. In 1988 more than 10 percent of the forest had been destroyed. The cutting goes on; so does burning, which produces gas that damages the ozone layer. More land has been lost to the flooding caused by the high dams, more than 900 square miles at Balbina. The mining process, notably the use of mercury in refining gold at Carajás, has contaminated rivers, poisoning goldminers and fish.

The economic gains have been disappointing. Most of the cleared land is unsuited for crops. Ludwig lost millions on the Jari project before he sold it at a loss. Much cut timber has been lost as a result of incompetence and corruption. The world market for pig iron collapsed, and the dams, for all their enormous cost, generate little electricity.

Finally, the schemes have done more harm than good in terms of people. Conflict broke out between the ranchers and the landless new arrivals, who wandered about the country with their families, occupying whatever land seemed vacant. According to a 1988 report by Amnesty International, more than a thousand were killed in less than eight years, and almost none of the killers were punished. Very few of

Rubber Tapper
in the Rain
Forest
Photo by
J. R. Ripper/
Imagens da Terra

the landless ever became independent small farmers as the
government had promised.

The ranchers also fought the *seringueiros* (rubber tappers),
who were descendants of Northeastern migrants who had in-
termarried with the Indians and made a living tapping wild
rubber trees in the forest. The *garimpeiros* (goldminers) at
Carajás fought with government forces when the government
tried to close the mines for repairs. Everyone fought with
the Indians, who resisted being deprived of their land, even
that allotted to them by the government. They also suffered
from mercury poisoning and other ills brought by "civilized"
Brazilian entrepreneurs.

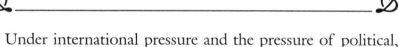

— *The Story of Chico Mendes* —

The struggle to preserve the rain forest is illustrated by the tragic true story of Chico Mendes. He was a *seringueiro* in the state of Acre who had learned to read and write. He organized other *seringueiros* to protest ranchers' efforts to cut down the forest and with it their livelihood. The method he used, *empate,* was a non-violent standoff in which large numbers of *seringueiros,* with their wives and children. would lie on the ground in front of the bulldozers and tractors that were to rip up the trees.

Realizing that broader efforts were needed, Chico worked with ecologically minded politicians and other environmentalists on a national campaign to make the public aware of the dangers to the rain forest and its people. He spoke to U.S. senators and the World Bank. He received a prize from the United Nations. His Union of the Rain Forest People made him world renowned but also made him enemies. One evening as he came out the back door of his little house, he was murdered. A film, *The Burning Season,* has been made of his life.

Under international pressure and the pressure of political, church, and other environmentalist groups, the Brazilian government has taken some measures to protect the Amazon rain forest. Some had already been written into the terms of its foreign loans. But all too often the measures do not go far enough or they are not enforced. Amazonia, like the dwindling areas of virgin forest in the United States and Canada, is still at risk.

Chapter 4

A "Christian People" and Other Gods

THE CHURCH IS A KITE

With three strips of wood, paper, and tenderness,
With a lot of string and a heap of love,
I make a kite and send it up
To dance in the sky like a multicolored dream.

This is the way the church is made:
Many people form a common Body
Filled with life, filled with hope,
Filled with love which makes the people one.

It is like the kite, which needs the wind
To fly to the sky and fill us with joy.
Only the Spirit gives life to the Church,
Calling it to move ahead, to love and to work.

—Song used in the Methodist Church in Brazil,
translated by Joyce Hill

*T*HE BRAZILIANS — Christians, Jews, Muslims, Buddhists, believers in African or Indian faiths — are a religious people in their strong sense of the spiritual world. Most of them consider themselves as part of a "Christian people," but they are many kinds of Christians. Often they mix their Christianity with other beliefs. It is this rich Christian brew that shapes religious life in Brazil.

The Roman Catholic Church

The Roman faith arrived in Brazil with the Portuguese, who regarded it as their mission to convert the Indians and then the Africans to Christianity. The pope gave the Portuguese king power to choose bishops and otherwise control the church in his domain. As the official religion, the church was tax exempt, but it was also under the Portuguese crown and then the Brazilian state. Generally the upper clergy and the great landowners and other leaders of society worked together to maintain their dominant position as a church and as a class, supporting slavery, controlling education, shaping Brazilian culture according to the conservative, patriarchal, Catholic worldview.

That worldview, as interpreted by the Portuguese, was more practical and easygoing than the rigid Spanish version. Many priests living in the countryside far from episcopal supervision or other priests, were looked after by housekeepers who often served as wives. Priests and bishops recognized that although most Portuguese men were married in church, they frequently disregarded its other teachings. Both clergy and laymen, however, insisted that Portuguese women should be good Catholics restricted to their homes and held to strict standards of conduct. Many devout women served the church faithfully in convents or in their local parishes.

The realistic, tolerant clergy usually overlooked the traditional religious practices that converted Indians and Africans carried over to their new faith. It was a short step from the

Celebrating the Feast of St. Anthony
Photo by Marcelo de Oliveira/Imagens da Terra

spirit-filled world of the African and Brazilian rain forests to the world of Catholic angels and saints. Processions, prayers, and promises of gifts in exchange for spiritual help could serve the new faith as well as the old. Carnival gained much from African and Indian love of music, dance, and spectacle. Catholic saints easily merged with the African *orixás*. African Catholics could venerate the Virgin Mary, Queen of Heaven, as the equivalent or replacement of Iemanjá, African Queen of the Waters. Similarly, St. Anne, mother of the Virgin, blended with Nana, mother of all the *orixás*, and the Devil was a close cousin of the troublemaking Exu. Thus believing people, living in poverty and oppression under their Portuguese masters, developed a kind of folk Catholicism that was a syncretism (mixture) of different religious elements.

The Roman Catholic Church began to lose its cultural dominance in the nineteenth century. Secularism and science, derived from Enlightenment ideas, and nationalism challenged its hold on people's minds and its close relation to the state and to the papacy. The government closed religious orders. There was a great shortage of Brazilian candidates for the priesthood, which meant that European and North American priests had to be imported. Often they had little understanding of the people. In the early twentieth century, the church was additionally challenged by communism and workers' movements, and it was separated from the state.

During these turbulent years, the Roman Catholic Church also lost its religious monopoly, as waves of Protestants arrived full of vitality and different religious, political, and social ideas. Today only 70 percent of the population calls itself Roman Catholic, and many of these, like Dom Antonio and Dona Josefina, are syncretists.

Protestant and Other Churches

Protestantism came to Brazil almost as early as Catholicism, but for three centuries it was only a trickle. Today its presence is considerable — 15 to 20 percent. Especially influential are the Pentecostal groups, which account for perhaps three out of every four Protestant Christians.

Immigrant Protestant Churches

In 1553 French Calvinists, or Huguenots, fleeing persecution by the Catholic kings of France, sought to establish a refuge on Guanabara Bay. Their ministers had time to draw up the Confessio Fulminensis ("Rio Confession"), the first Protestant confession of faith in the New World, before they were expelled by the Portuguese in 1567.

In 1624 Dutch Protestant colonists settled in the Northeastern coastal provinces of Paraíba and Pernambuco. They brought the Dutch Reformed Church, organizing presbyteries and baptizing converts to this Dutch Calvinist faith. The Portuguese drove them out in 1654 and barbarously persecuted converts who remained.

Because Portugal was under obligation to Britain, the leading imperial power after the defeat of Napoleon, Portugal had to allow Britons traveling in Brazil to establish churches for Anglican worship. The first one was founded in Rio in 1824. Of course, the government did not allow anyone but British to attend its services.

About the same time, the Brazilian government permitted German immigrants to the Southeastern highlands to establish Lutheran churches, provided only Germans attended and the services were in German. In 1950 these immigrant churches became the Evangelical Church of Lutheran Confession in Brazil.

Thus Anglicanism and Lutheranism were the greater part of so-called immigrant Protestantism, which later included other groups such as the Hungarian Reformed Church and the Arab Presbyterian Church.

Missionary Protestant Churches

In the mid-nineteenth century, Protestant churches in the United States began sending missionaries to Brazil and other parts of the world. The first Methodists arrived in 1836 but failed. Slaveholding Southern Methodists who emigrated to Brazil after the Civil War founded a Methodist church in 1871. Methodist missionaries came to aid them and convert Brazilians. Meanwhile a Scottish Congregational missionary and his wife arrived in 1855 and Presbyterians in 1859. Baptists opened their first church in 1881. The American Episcopalian Church founded a mission in 1889 in Rio do Sul, working in a different area from the older Anglican Church. The Seventh-day Adventists arrived in 1900. Non-Protestant missionaries were sent by the Church of Jesus Christ of Latter-day Saints (Mormons) and Jehovah's Witnesses.

These mainstream Protestant and other missions were founded, supported, and run by denominational headquarters in the United States. They brought with them new ideas — the value of personal reading of the Bible, self-reliance and self-government, and self-improvement through education and hard work. They encouraged political reform. At the same time, they sternly disapproved of drinking, smoking, dancing, gambling, and sex out of wedlock. These values reflected the liberal democratic society taking shape in the United States. They attracted some middle-class Brazilians, including Free Masons and army officers who were already inclined toward science and secularism, and a few lower-class Brazilians who adopted Protestant values as a way to move into the middle class. But such values were quite foreign to the tolerant, pleasure-loving Brazilians who formed the aristocracy and the bulk of the lower class.

Reflecting their emphasis on Bible reading and education, the Protestant missions founded a network of schools from the primary level to university. These schools, which introduced new teaching methods and included practical subjects such as science and technology, were highly regarded in a country where there were often no public schools beyond third grade and very few secondary schools. They were attended by both Protestants and Catholics. Notable examples are Colégio Bennett (for girls) in Rio, the agricultural college in Lavras, and the Presbyterian commercial college in São Paulo that became Mackenzie University. Through their schools the Protestants contributed to the weakening of the conservative aristocratic pattern of society carried over from colonial times.

Throughout their history in Brazil, almost all the Protestant churches were also concerned about the situation of the poor and involved in ministry with them. They founded orphanages for abandoned children, day-care centers for children of working mothers, and social centers offering opportunities for group activity and skills training in urban areas. These programs were designed to meet im-

Feeding the Poor in São Paulo
Photo by Richard Lord

mediate needs, but there was no accompanying analysis of the causes of the problems or development of strategies for changing the system that kept the poor in their poverty. Protestants found it difficult to overcome a minority complex, surrounded as they were by the majority culture of Roman Catholicism; so the programs were usually small and designed to encourage the participants to become active members of the Protestant churches.

Indeed, until after World War II, these mission Protestants believed that to be a Protestant in Brazil was to be virulently anti-Catholic. Along with Catholic theology and church structure, they also opposed the basic culture of the people they were trying to evangelize because of its links to Catholic practices. Divorced from cultural reality and unable to mold a new concept of the church, they failed to reach all but a few of the common people and eventually lost some of their appeal for the middle class.

Pentecostal Churches

Pentecostalism, a conservative fundamentalist movement in Protestantism, developed in rural areas of the United States in the early twentieth century. It inspired a number of missionaries who carried its message around the world. Two Swedish-born missionaries from Chicago founded the Assemblies of God in Belém in 1911. The Assemblies spread rapidly throughout the country, becoming the largest Pentecostal body and maintaining a seminary and publishing house. About the same time, Luigi Francescon, an Italian-born missionary living in Chicago, founded the Christian Congregation of Brazil among Italian immigrants in the South. Another U.S. missionary founded the Church of the Foursquare Gospel in 1946, which soon became independent of its American origins. In the wake of these three groups, many others appeared.

Pentecostalists generally downplayed centralized church government and an educated clergy, valued by many mainstream Protestant churches, and were not involved in political or social issues. Instead they stressed personal piety that would lead to a reward in heaven and on earth experiences of religious ecstasy, including speaking in tongues.

Indian and African Religions

Despite Brazil's long Christian history, it must be remembered that Christianity was a foreign import imposed on indigenous peoples, African slaves, and the subsequent mixtures by force of arms and economic power. It was presented as "truth" to peoples who already had their own religious beliefs and practices. Just as the European conquerors slaughtered Indians and Africans who opposed them, they also tried to destroy their faith, refusing to understand it and condemning it as a work of the Devil. Slaves were baptized, sometimes even before leaving Africa. In the baptismal ceremony they were branded with an iron that left a scar in the form of the cross and the Portuguese crown, indicating not only that the slave was baptized but that the owner had paid the appropriate tax. Worship of African deities (the *orixás*) was forbidden.

As we have seen, the church appeared to triumph, but it was not a conclusive victory. Despite persecution by the police, which continued until the 1940s, Indians and Africans continued to practice their faith in secret, calling on the spirits of nature or their ancestors to help them in time of need. As Catholic converts, they borrowed Catholic saints and other beliefs for their own religions, and they brought much of their own faith into the church with them. Today the oppressed people present an amalgam of faiths. Very few are completely Christian or completely animist, as Christians describe believers in a world of spirits. Most people are a bit of both.

Indian Shamans and the Spirit World

According to Harold Osburne, author of *South American Mythology*, the Indians of the rain forest had no temples, statues, or public religious ceremonies. They believed in a supernatural world of spirits who personified the sun and moon, mountains, streams, and other elements of nature or tribal ancestors. The shaman knew how to call on them for help to cure the sick, send hunting animals or rain for the crops, or foretell the future. He conducted special rituals to mark social status, coming of age and other rites of passage, and roles of men and women. The shaman also preserved tribal traditions and encouraged respect for the spirits and the land on which the tribe's welfare depended.

African Priestesses and the Orixás

Slaves from different parts of Africa brought different religions with them. The Bantus believed in Zumbi, the supreme god, and *egums,* the wandering souls of their ancestors. The Yorubas had a more formalized faith headed by Oloum ("Heaven"), the supreme god, who was reached only indirectly through the *orixás* (identified with forces of nature). As the various African peoples were mixed together and scattered through Brazil, they simplified their worship to find common elements. Of the more than 400 *orixás* in Africa, they retained only about a dozen. At the same time they developed a variety of religious expressions. Today African religions flourish openly. They attract especially lower-class city Brazilians, but many middle-class and upper-class Brazilians believe as well.

Three African-based faiths are notable. *Candomblé,* the most purely African, is strongest in the Northeast, where the most Africans are. *Macumba,* which combines *candomblé* with Indian and Catholic elements, is influential in Rio. *Umbanda,* prevalent in the Southeastern highlands, is a syncretistic mixture of African and Catholic elements with the teachings of Alain Kardec, a nineteenth-century Frenchman who founded a cult devoted to communication with spiritual beings in outer space.

Joseph A. Page, author of *The Brazilians* (1995), describes a *candomblé terreiro* ("land"), or temple. It includes a large meeting hall or courtyard with shrines for two *orixás* and an altar for Catholic saints. It has also quarters for the ruling priestess or priest ("mother, or father, of sainthood") and lesser officials and shrines for other *orixás.* Two of the most important *orixás* are Iemanjá, Queen of the Waters (Virgin Mary) and Oxala, Lord of the Good End (the baby Jesus). There are also the children of Iemanjá — Xango, god of lightning (St. Jerome); Ogun, god of the hunt and war (St. Anthony or St. George); and Exu, messenger between the *orixás* and humans and troublemaker. Attached to each *terreiro* are patrons (often socially important whites) and initiates ("daughters, or sons, of sainthood"), who go through special ceremonies that enable them to be possessed by their personal *orixá.*

A *candomblé* service, according to Page, is preceded by a sacrifice of a goat or chicken or other food and a communal meal. Only initiates take part. The main service, open to all worshipers and guests, begins with a procession of the initiates, in costume, dancing and singing in the Yoruba language to the beat of drums. In the course of the service they are entered ("mounted") by their *orixás,* causing them to shake and shout and twirl and fall down. Such religious ecstasy offers a way for initiates to escape a harsh reality through identification with a god. At other times believers consult with the priestess, who conveys advice from the *orixás.* Believers bring offerings to the *terreiro* or leave them at crossroads. They may wear a necklace or carry an amulet sacred to their *orixá.*

Candomblé does not teach moral lessons or invite believers to a better life in the next world. Instead it proclaims that life in this world has value. In the words of the Brazilian scholars M. Barros Souza and J. L. Caravias, it celebrates earth and nature. In addition, as noted by M. Bergman, *candomblé* gives the poor a sense of community and a dignity that society denies them.

It is a pity that the Brazilian theological, liturgical, and community experience did not have deeper repercussions on the life of the Christian churches. Both Catholics and Protestants tried to give Brazilians a Latin or Anglo-Saxon version of the gospel and the church that was more in tune with the oppressive forces of society than the needs and tastes of the people.

Chapter 5

Brazilian Response to Need

CHALLENGE
AND COMMITMENT

There is nothing to fear
except to join the struggle.
There is nothing to do
except forget our fears.

In your hands, O God,
we place our lives.
And we offer them
as instruments of truth and justice.
Transform our weakness into strength,
our timidity into courage.
Teach us day by day
to trust in you and in your care,
so that our hearts will be filled with sincerity,

and the bonds of solidarity and community
will be strengthened among all your people.

— Ernesto Barros Cardoso,
translated by Joyce Hill

*T*HE END of World War II, the struggle between capitalism and communism for world supremacy, and the
radicalism of the 1960s brought many changes in social and
religious thinking in North America and Brazil. Some Americans became more critical of their own capitalist society, less
superior in their attitude toward the rest of the world, and
more aware of the needs of their mission churches. Brazilian churches became more aware of the needs of the people,
both within denominations and as part of a broad ecumenical
movement.

The Roman Catholic Church

In the 1950s and early 1960s the Roman Catholic Church
across Latin America began to move into a new, closer relationship with the common people. It broadened its concept
of "being the Church" as the ideal savior of souls and practical ally of the rich and the military to being "the voice of the
voiceless," committed to helping the poor obtain social justice. Some clergy, influenced by Marxism, organized workers
and peasants and set up literacy classes.

It rapidly became clear that traditional theological answers
were no longer adequate to meet the new demands on the
church. The church needed to be set free to find new direc-
tions in biblical study, liturgy, and especially its action in the
world. It needed to find new wineskins for this new wine.

This new spirit was expressed in the Second Vatican Council (1962–1965), called by Pope John XXIII, which stressed
social justice, involvement of the laity (the people), and ecumenical cooperation. The new spirit also emerged in Latin
America as liberation theology. In the words of the Francis-

can friar Leonardo Boff, its spokesman in Brazil, liberation theology meant a new vision of the church being "born of the people by the breath of the Spirit." The faith of the people was to create a new, just, anticapitalist society.

As the largest national Roman Catholic Church in the world, the church in Brazil has done more than any other to meet the challenge presented by what it means to be the church today. It set up pastoral commissions to deal with the land, the indigenous, workers, children, and other areas of need.

Unfortunately, some more traditional clergy resisted these new, political views. Pope John Paul II, although sympathetic to the poor, opposes any suggestion of Marxism; he has forbidden Boff to write or teach. The military government, which took over Brazil in 1964, lost no time in suppressing any voices, including church voices, perceived to be a threat to a stable, capitalist state. "Radical" clergy were beaten or shot. Many people in opposition began to "disappear." Two outstanding churchmen, Dom Hélder Câmara, archbishop of Recife, and Cardinal Dom Paulo Evaristo Arns of São Paulo, spoke out boldly in favor of social justice and against this trampling of human rights. Dom Paulo published a carefully researched book detailing the torture of political prisoners by the military government. Other churchmen opened the door to ecumenical ventures by helping found the National Council of Churches of Brazil (discussed later in this chapter). The church even challenged all Christians in Brazil to consider a "macro-ecumenity," which would include African and Indian religions.

Mainstream Protestant Churches

Many of Brazil's missionary Protestant churches have become independent of foreign headquarters in matters of internal structure and governance. Traditional ministries continue. The People's Institute, a social center in Rio, has just celebrated its hundredth anniversary. Many of the established ministries are being expanded to meet increasing needs, and new programs for emerging needs have been created. Programs with urban poor and other marginalized people often still continue to receive financial assistance, which might come from the World Council of Churches, the National Council of Churches of Christ in the USA, or the headquarters of the founding church.

— From Scavengers to Community —

Over the last three years, Pastor Anna has been making regular visits to a group of families who scrape a living sorting garbage on a huge heap that has accumulated on the outskirts of São Bernardo, near São Paulo. City dump trucks drive up the hill of refuse so frequently that people have to move fast to sort out the salvage before the next load arrives. Everyone works, even small children. Some sort out glass, others paper, or metal, or cast off clothing, which they sell to dealers. Because they are paid by weight, they can't stop working very long at one time.

When Pastor Anna first appeared, she found each family working on its own. Through her visits, they have gradually formed a community, which looks out for all its members. They have set aside part of the dump to grow vegetables, which they toss in a common soup pot for the mid-day meal they share. They have set up a covered child-care area at one side of the dump where an older girl watches the babies and smallest children. As Pastor Anna talks to each family while they work, new light shines in their eyes, and they feel reassured, knowing they are not forgotten. Because she has helped them find dignity as children of God, they can all rejoice when one of them, Ignacio, finds a "real job," washing dishes in a restaurant downtown.

Mainstream Protestant churches have also joined forces with one another in ecumenical ventures, notably the Latin America Council of Churches (CLAI), which met in Brazil in 1988.

— *Joy in Solidarity* —

At the opening session of CLAI, a bishop was handed a telegram: "Roberto arrested in demonstration of landless peasants." Although the Constitution of 1988 protects productive land from expropriation, it does not define "productive." Therefore a small garden on a large tract of land protects the owner, despite the need of thousands of peasants for a small plot of their own. Roberto, one of the bishop's pastors, had taken part in a week-long sit-in by peasants in a pasture on the outskirts of Linhares in central Brazil. The bishop immediately

Squatter with Her Family
Photo by Everaldo Rocha/Imagens da Terra

told the assembly what had happened and prepared to depart.

"You are not going alone!" the delegates bravely replied. Carrying out the theme of the meeting, "Hope in Solidarity," they prepared a letter for the bishop to take with him. It protested the arrest of Roberto and the peasant leaders, and it was signed by more than 600 names.

The delegates also called their home countries. Soon calls from Brazil and abroad in solidarity with the peasants flooded Linhares. The mayor and police were overwhelmed. When the bishop arrived, they immediately offered to release Pastor Roberto. He refused to leave without the peasant leaders. The landowners pressed the mayor to keep them all in jail. After all, they had invaded private property. Meanwhile, the rest of the peasants were still sitting in the pasture. It was a standoff for several days. Finally international pressure from the churches of CLAI prevailed. When the jail doors opened, pastor and peasants walked out together. Shortly before the closing session of the CLAI, the assembly received a telegram from Roberto's bishop announcing the release. Instantaneously the theme "Hope in Solidarity" became "Joy in Solidarity!"

Another Protestant ecumenical venture is the Evangelical Missionary Task Force, which encourages Protestant churches in Brazil to find ways to be in solidarity with Indian groups.

— The Safest Clams —

A tiny, poor congregation in a little fishing village near Fortaleza on the Northeast coast pondered what it could do to demonstrate solidarity with the rapidly shrinking community of Potiguara Indians, who lived nearby.

Rich people in Fortaleza had built weekend homes along the village's tranquil beach, but they did not want the Potiguaras, who made their living raising and digging clams, to walk on the beach. The Potiguaras contested the invasion of their land, which they had occupied for centuries, but the houses continued to go up, and Fortaleza declared that the area that had been set aside for the Potiguaras years before had never really been their homeland.

The congregation thought that this problem was a way they could show solidarity with the Potiguaras. Carlos, a church member, asked his uncle, who worked in city hall, to do some checking. Tio Pedro discovered that the contested land had indeed been established as a reservation for the Potiguaras, and he copied the documents to prove it. It would be hard to say who was more delighted when the congregation invited Chief Irineu to church and presented him with the papers.

It wasn't long, however, before newspapers, radio, and television were spreading the word that the clams were so polluted that they were not safe to eat. The Potiguaras were indignant. They knew the clams did not make them or anyone else sick, and they had always sold out early in the Fortaleza market. Nevertheless, householders organized a boycott.

This time church members asked Chief Irineu how they could help. Neither the Indians nor the congregation could afford an engineer to test the waters, but Rosa asked her neighbor, João, who was an environmental engineer, to help. The rest of the congregation prayed, and João said yes! His tests discovered that the polluted waters were all south of the Potiguaras' land in an area of beach houses that had no adequate sewer system.

Newspaper and television reports of the test results were dramatic, but the most emotional moment of solidarity was when the congregation joined hands with the Potiguaras to march through the city of Fortaleza to the market. They all carried placards announcing that the safest place to buy fresh clams, from the purest stretch of Atlantic Ocean front, was the Potiguara stand in the market.

Pentecostal Churches

The rapid industrialization of Brazil in the 1950s and 1960s and the economic problems of the succeeding decades created a vast need among the urban poor. A new crop of Pentecostal churches sprang up to fill it. According to one survey, noted by Page, a new Protestant church opened in Rio every day, and nine out of ten were Pentecostal. According to another authority, one Brazilian in six is Pentecostal.

These churches offered emotional services that stressed faith healing and other benefits to be gained through exorcising the Devil. They also stressed self-improvement through moral behavior, education, and hard work. Churches helped members find jobs, and making money was considered a sign of being a good Christian. Pentecostalism had great appeal for poor city dwellers, accustomed to faith healing and spirit possession in Indian and African traditions and needing a sense of community to replace the family ties in the countryside they had left behind.

The new Pentecostals also were quick to use modern methods of communication. The Universal Church of the Kingdom of God, founded by Edir Macedo in 1977, reaches millions through mass rallies at soccer stadiums or on the radio and television. The church preaches the importance of faith, expressed by solid financial contributions, which Bishop Macedo, as he is called, controls. Unlike other Pentecostal churches, the Universal Church does not ask members to give up smoking, drinking, and dancing — basic pleasures in the lives of many Brazilians. Page estimates the church may have 2 million members in more than 800 congregations. It has sent missionaries to cities in other countries, including Brooklyn, New York. At the same time the charismatic bishop has also built a business empire that includes a large television network, much in the style of United States televangelists. Questions have arisen about tax evasion and possible misuse of funds.

The new Pentecostal churches are far more concerned than the older ones about social problems. Brazil for Christ, founded by Manoel de Mello in 1956, was one of the first to call for social justice. Almost all have participated in the National Campaign Against Hunger, a program aided by churches, organizations, individuals, city government, and even the operators of the illegal numbers game. (The Universal Church organized its own campaign.) They have also participated in a program to reduce the increasing violence in Rio. The Pentecostals can no longer be written off as nonparticipants in society.

Unlike the otherworldly older Pentecostals, the new ones, after the departure of the military government, are taking a political role. They have discovered that political action is one way of achieving social justice. Some Pentecostals, even some pastors, have been candidates for public office. Their conservative presence in Congress (they oppose abortion) has created tensions among other Protestants, especially over the proposed formation of a Christian political party.

The Pentecostals are not generally inclined toward ecumenism. They are usually more interested in winning converts than in joining ecumenical movements with the Roman Catholic Church or African religions. Some have physically attacked *terreiros*.

National Council of Christian Churches of Brazil

As the Roman Catholic Church became more open toward Protestants, some Protestant denominations were able to overcome their anti-Catholic feelings and find ways to work with Catholics on specific problems. These programs have received both human and financial resources from the National Council of Churches of Christ in the USA, the United Church of Canada, and the Anglican Church of Canada. Such cooperation led the Lutheran Church, the Methodist Church, the Episcopal Church, the Christian Reformed Church, and the United Presbyterian Church to join with the Roman Catholic Church to found the National Council of Christian Churches in Brazil (CONIC) in 1982. CONIC is the only national council of churches in South America in which Protestants and Catholics work together on council activities. From its beginning CONIC has endeavored to promote human dignity and human rights for all persons who seek love, justice, and peace. Two of its concerns are combatting AIDS and racism.

Consultation on HIV and AIDS

Several years ago, if a church member were asked to describe how the church was responding to the pandemic of HIV and AIDS, the response would probably have been, "It isn't." In fact, many churches considered HIV and AIDS as something that has no business in the daily life of a church. For many, however, it became evident that the church could not continue to ignore the fact that the virus was not only real but was also present in the families of its members. This view was reflected in the words of Maria Luiza, a Presbyterian: "I believe that my church wants to be in solidarity with those who carry the HIV/AIDS virus. I also believe that my church is looking for ways to be involved. I think that it is concerned, knowing that it is urgent to be prepared to deal with this issue in order to carry out a ministry of support."

KOINONIA (an ecumenical ministry discussed later), supported by CONIC, organized and promoted the Consultation on HIV and AIDS. Accordingly, official representatives of CONIC and the Roman Catholic, Methodist, Free Methodist, Lutheran, Independent Presbyterian, United Presbyterian, Presbyterian Church of Brazil, and Anglican churches gathered in São Paulo in November 1995. Representatives from government health-care programs provided professional data. Together the church leaders considered the pastoral challenge of HIV and AIDS. They acknowledged that they faced not just a medical problem but one with ethical aspects that the churches had not adequately addressed. The participants agreed that they should work ecumenically wherever possible to avoid duplication of efforts. They learned of the programs already developed, such as the homes for those with HIV and AIDS run by the Catholic Church in several parts of the country. They shared the materials that were already being used by the Methodists. They committed themselves to work together in programs of solidarity with those who are victims of HIV and AIDS and their families. Before the consultation was over, they took steps to create a network of persons in local churches — doctors, social workers, nurses, sociologists, and pastors — who were already working with the problem. They agreed to recruit others to become more involved.

Mose Ramos Neto, a Presbyterian pastor who spends part of his time as a chaplain in the Emilio Ribas Hospital in São Paulo, was encouraged by the consultation: "We must have a spirit of unity among us to consider the problem of HIV/AIDS. So far we have not been able to find a cure, but by pooling our energies and ideas and putting aside our dogmas and preconceived prejudices, I am convinced that we will begin to solve the problem."

Combatting Racism

Through its Committee to Combat Racism (CENACORA), CONIC is working to help restore a sense of pride among Brazil's black population. The so-called democracy has been challenged by emerging black organizations who point out that darker-skinned people find it harder than whites to obtain well-paying jobs and receive lower wages for the same work. Few blacks in Brazil receive the minimum wage (about US$135 a month). Most of the slum dwellers are black, and they have a higher illiteracy rate than whites.

CENACORA has more than twenty staff persons throughout the country trying to open communication between different racial sectors of society. It holds seminars and workshops to help blacks develop pride in their cultural heritage. Creating a black theology that takes into account African religious expressions is more difficult because Protestants generally reject their validity. Nevertheless, CENACORA is seeking ways that the adherents of *candomblé* and *umbanda* can be included in the dialogues, knowing that without them, no meaningful work can be done.

Ecclesial Base Communities

Small grass-roots communities of Christian laypeople appeared in Brazil first among Catholics, then among Protestants. They are called by several names: Ecclesial Base Communities, Christian Base Communities, and Grass-roots Christian Communities. In this book they will be referred to by their Brazilian acronym, CEBs, for Comunidades Eclesiais de Base.

In the Roman Catholic Church

In 1956 in Northeast Brazil, an old woman challenged her bishop, Dom Agnelo Rossi: "At Christmas the three Protestant churches were lit up and filled with people. We could hear their singing. But our Catholic church was closed and dark because no priest came to celebrate the Mass." As the conservative bishop reflected on these words, he began to develop a plan to help the life of the parishes where there were not enough priests. Little did he know that his plan would alter the life and witness of the Roman Catholic Church not only in Brazil but throughout Latin America.

According to the bishop's plan, priests, nuns, teachers in parochial schools, and catechists were trained to encourage the local parishes to engage in Bible study, prayer, and discussion on how to live their faith from day to day. In each group a person was selected to be responsible not only for spiritual assistance to the members but also for initiating social-service projects and developing life together in the congregation. Thus the Ecclesial Base Communities were born. They fit the guidelines set at Vatican II, which opened the church to new ways of expressing one's faith. They also filled the need of the many parishes that had no resident priest. According to Leonardo Boff, they created a new way of "being the Church." Dom Hélder Câmara and Dom Paulo Arns provided strong leadership for the movement. In 1965 the Brazilian National Conference of Bishops affirmed the existence of the CEBs, and the Latin American Bishops Conference held in Medellín, Colombia, in 1969, heralded them as a sign of hope for the renewal of the church in Latin America.

In order to understand the reasons for the success of the CEBs, especially in the 1980s, one must look into the history of the Brazilian church. In Brazil the church had never entirely managed to adopt the central structure of the church in Europe or North America. Because of the lack of priests and nuns, the church could not develop according to the model that was imported from abroad. The laity always played an important role in the church organization. So the CEBs are the expression of an old tradition, a form of grass-roots organization at the heart of the people's life.

Springing up primarily among the poor, the CEBs clearly choose to address the concerns of society's impoverished and excluded. From a theological perspective, they try to bring the gospel to life by relating it to the concrete reality of oppression in which the people live. As a number of CEBs say, "We have understood that the Church is ourselves when we seek to improve our living conditions and those of our community, to help improve the situation of our people."

Obviously such an endeavor makes headway only amidst many tensions and conflicts. The use of the Bible is not always clear and unequivocal, and its relationship to an analysis of reality is sometimes arbitrary and confused. Still, this dimension is basic to the revitalizing of community life and introduces the way that many Brazilian Catholics are the church.

The national meetings of the CEBs reveal their strength. Only seventy persons from eleven dioceses attended the first meeting in 1975 under the theme "A Church Born of the People by the Spirit of God." By 1986, the sixth meeting was visibly ecumenical with Protestant participation on all levels. Two hundred four dioceses sent 1,623 delegates to that meeting, whose theme was "The People of God Seeking the Promised Land." Participation increased still more at the eighth meeting in 1992, where 2,326 delegates from 314 dioceses discussed the theme "The People of God Reborn in Oppressed Cultures." The ninth meeting, slated for July 1997, will consider the CEBs as "Life and Hope Among the People." More than 2,000 participants, Catholic and Protestant, are expected to work together on indigenous cultures, Pentecostalism, popular religions, and solidarity with the excluded of society.

The CEBs, which developed at the same time as the repressive military dictatorship, provided one of the few opportunities for the people to meet and talk together. As the participants realized the link between their faith, scriptures, and their daily activity, many of the CEBs became highly politicized in considering options for their lives. This tendency caused conservative bishops and other church leaders to become highly critical of the CEBs and to accuse them of being Marxist cell groups or communist fronts. Their fate was uncertain at their Puebla, Mexico, meeting in 1979. However, the Brazilian bishops who staunchly defended the CEBs prevailed. The conference reaffirmed its mission to reflect a "preferential option for the poor," that is, to work with the landless, the indigenous, the workers, and others excluded from the existing social and economic structures.

Since then the Roman Catholic Church has been growing more conservative. The Vatican has appointed more conservative bishops. The one who replaced the retiring Dom Hélder dismantled most of the structures Dom Hélder had created. The powerful archdiocese of São Paulo was subdivided, reducing the influence of Dom Paulo. The 1992 meeting of the Latin American Bishops in the Dominican Republic backed off from its former progressive stance. Nevertheless, the CEBs have opened new windows that will not be closed, though they may be reshaped. For, as a local leader expressed it, "Once you squeeze toothpaste out of the tube, you cannot put it back in."

In the Protestant Churches

Protestant churches have not been strangers to the effects of Roman Catholic CEBs on the life of the poor. Moreover, the historical Protestant experience in many ways makes Protestants sympathetic to the CEBs. It is important to recognize first that non-Catholic churches of every denomination are essentially small communities. Even the large Pentecostal churches are organized in small groups for prayer, Bible study, and fellowship. Second, Brazilian Protestantism, in general, is profoundly anticlerical; its churches emphasize the rule of the laity and the importance of the local community. The regional and national organization of the church is not so important. Some scholars go so far as to say that Brazil's religion is basically congregational Protestantism. The believer's horizon of the church is the horizon of the local congregation. Third, the Bible has been the trademark of Protestants in Brazil for more than a century and a half, although it was read more for spiritual truth than for any direct reference to the specific historical situations of the people's experience. From the Protestant perspective, the rise of the

CEBs might be called the Protestantization of the Catholic parish experience. The difference lies in the concept of the meaning, rationale, and mission of the CEBs in their social context. For Catholics, what matters is that the church, as an institution, be present with its proposals and perhaps with its leadership in the political processes of society. For Protestants of all kinds, what matters is that Christians as members of a faith community be good persons and good citizens who share in the political life of their society as individuals, never as an organized community or institutional church.

These assertions are only generalizations, of course, and are subject to many variations. It is possible to find highly spiritualistic and charismatic CEBs, almost Pentecostal in attitude, just as it is possible to find small Protestant congregations that are deeply politicized and more involved in the struggles of the people than many Catholic communities.

— *Dona Amelia's Faith* —

Dona Amelia, a member of a Presbyterian congregation in a Rio *favela*, shared how she lives her faith in these words:

"Here in our church, encouraged by Jesus' example and inspired by His Spirit, we understand that to preach the Gospel or bear witness to Jesus is to serve the people who share with us the problems and difficulties of our *favelas*. From the moment we began to join together as Presbyterians, we have realized that service to others is an essential part of our church's task. So we have always combined our commitment to preaching and concerted action of the church with other groups within the *favela*.

"As a result we are respected, and the people who live here know they can rely on us in any situation. From the creation of the Neighborhood Committee more than twenty years ago up to now, our church has always taken sides with the interests of the more than 60,000 suffering people who live here.

"It is known that Rio de Janeiro has over 600 *favelas*. ...About a third of the population are virtually imprisoned in these miserable living conditions. Here we have shared memorable battles for electricity, drinking water, better public transportation, garbage collection, and ownership of the small plots of land. Thanks to God and to the spirit of struggle of so many brothers and sisters, we have won all of these struggles in the last fifteen years. Our small church has always been in the forefront of all of the struggles, sometimes in concert with the municipal authorities and sometimes against them. They now respect us and seek out collaboration.

"Our sisters and brothers in other denominations, and even some members of other congregations of our own church, criticize us at times, telling us that we are not converting people with this work...that we are doing things that have nothing to do with the Gospel, which is essentially [about] salvation for sinners...that we ought to leave what we are doing to the authorities. We pay no attention to these criticisms. For us, to serve people is the Great Commission of the Gospel. If others, conscienticized by the way we are the Church and live our faith, want to join us, of course, we welcome them."

While the primary purpose of the CEBs and their equivalent groups in the Protestant and Pentecostal churches is to engage in Bible study and prayer, their actions differ. The CEBs appear to be living out their mission, exemplifying the "preferential option for the poor," even as the church leadership becomes more conservative. Protestants and Pentecostals don't want to rock the boat and lose the social and economic gains their members have achieved. Both groups have the potential to be the leaven in the lump, bringing new life and hope to the excluded of society.

— *The Word of God with the People of God* —

On a hot Friday morning, in the main plaza of Trinidade, a town near Brasília, almost 10,000 delegates and workers were gathered for the Mass celebrating the close of a national assembly of CEBs. Just before the Mass started, a coffee picker in a faded cotton dress and plastic thong sandals carrying a large Bible worked her way into the midst of the crowd. The Mass began. When it was time to read the Gospel, the reader, who was a Protestant woman pastor, stepped to the empty lectern. When the officiating Catholic priest in his vestments asked, "Where is the Word of God?" the woman in the crowd lifted the Bible over her head for all to see.

The people responded, "The Word of God is with the people of God." The priest proclaimed, "Let the Word of God come to us from the people of God." The people then passed the big Bible forward, over their heads, to the hands of the priest, who opened it to the Gospel and handed it to the pastor. She read the words of Jesus back to the people from whom the Word had come.

Ministries with Street Children

In 1981 more than 900 pastors, bishops, and lay persons concerned about the plight of children met together in the First Ecumenical Week of the Child. They came from Lutheran, Methodist, Presbyterian, Anglican, and Roman Catholic churches to affirm that their faith demanded commitment to the oppressed and suffering children. These churches had begun a ministry among street children as individual denominations. This meeting laid the groundwork for the Pastoral Commission for Children in the Roman Catholic Church and the expansion of the ministry with children in the Protestant churches. These leaders, together with persons from UNICEF, government agencies, labor unions, and the children themselves, worked to organize the National Movement of Street Children. In 1986 it took children from the major cities of Brazil by bus to Brasília, where Congress was drafting a new Constitution. The children discussed their needs and proposed their own solutions. They requested an opportunity to talk with government leaders to present their recommendations. Gathering in one of the marble-floored chambers of the capitol, they posed several questions:

Why do you live in splendor (*luxo*) while we live in squalor (*lixo*)?

Is it legal for the police to demand sexual favors from the girls when they are arrested? If so, change the law.

Is it legal for the police to beat the children they detain? If so, change the law.

Is it legal to arrest us without telling us what charges are being brought against us? If so, change the law.

These concerns were addressed in Article 207 of the new Constitution of 1988:

> When a child commits a crime, measures to assure his/her rehabilitation will be taken. Therefore, he/she must receive special treatment. No one shall be beaten or mistreated. When a child or adolescent is taken prisoner, it is necessary that he/she know the reason. (paragraph 3, v)
>
> The government authorities shall develop programs to prevent addiction to drugs or other narcotics and shall severely punish crimes of sexual abuse and exploitation committed against children and adolescents. (paragraph 4, vii)

By 1990, the National Movement of Street Children was organized in twenty-two of Brazil's twenty-seven states with more than 3,000 volunteers working to defend the rights of the children. Unfortunately, the new constitution has not been enforced, so children are still victims and continue to be at risk. Bishop Isac Aco, president of CONIC, wrote, "We can delay no longer. It is a matter of life or death for the Children and for Brazil. It is also a matter of faith."

Street Children, a "National Priority"
Photo by Nando Neves/Imagens da Terra

Alarmed by the increase of violent deaths among street children, the National Movement for Street Children and the Brazilian Institute for Social and Economic Analysis (IBASE) studied the problem in 1989. They were able to document 1,397 violent deaths in sixteen states, verified by the Legal

Medical Institute of Brazil. An Amnesty International report quotes from a 1991 Parliamentary Commission of Inquiry, which confirmed that in 1990 there were 427 homicides against children and adolescents under eighteen.

> Most of the killings were carried out by death squads, in many cases integrated by off-duty police officers, usually hired by local shopkeepers to "clean up" the area.... The Commission found evidence that suggested police and judiciary authorities' involvement with death squads and the report gives examples of specific cases.

Two years later IBASE and three other agencies revisited the problem. Their research showed that the primary victims between 1991 and 1993 were not "street children" but poor teenage boys whose deaths were probably drug related. These agencies recommended that the authorities in Rio create in poor neighborhoods programs of job training, sports, music, and other arts that would provide the boys with other options for their lives.

Such programs are being sponsored by many churches, which cooperate in the National Ecumenical Ministry with Street Children. A Roman Catholic program in Belém, called the Little Street Vendors' Republic, offers training in mechanical skills and help in setting up cooperatives. A Methodist program in São Paulo sponsors a Shoeshiners' Cooperative and classes in metalwork, candy making, and silkscreening on T shirts and cards. It also offers classes in *capoeira*, a warlike dance developed by African slaves, as a way of giving black boys a sense of pride in their heritage and a way to earn money giving performances that people pay to see.

— Need a Shine? —

"Hey, Mister! Need a shine?" Marcos squatted down on his shoe shine box beside a man on his lunch break who was reading the paper on a bench in front of the Cathedral of São Paulo. Startled, he looked at the small shoe shiner, checked his watch, and asked, "Why aren't you in school?"

"I do go to school," replied Marcos, "but not the way you mean." Then he explained that he belonged to the Shoe Shiners' Cooperative, where he learned to share responsibility and decision making. As a member he also attended an alternative school, mobile classes held on strips of old carpet that were moved from street to street to reach different students. There he learned reading and arithmetic, basic skills that helped him check prices of shoe polish and brushes and determine how much to charge for a shoe shine in order to make a profit. He also learned his rights as a child guaranteed by the Constitution. He was proud of his older friend, Juvenil, who in 1986 had gone on a bus to Brasília with other children to talk to Congress.

The man received more than a shoe shine. Before he returned to work he had learned that street children can have dignity, a sense of self-worth, and the ability to work together when someone cares enough to make it happen. Such programs are barely a drop in the bucket in terms of the great need, but they change the lives of the individuals they reach, and they show what can be done.

Other Ecumenical Ministries

Catholics and Protestants cooperate on a number of other ministries to meet the people's needs.

The Ecumenical Center for Services to Evangelization and Popular Education

A Roman Catholic layman from the Northeast, Paulo Freire, believed that illiterate people could learn to read if they understood that reading and writing could help them escape poverty and social rejection. His concept of popular education used a multi-disciplinary approach in which all aspects of life are seen as part of the process of education. Participants are not passive recipients but contribute to the process and learn from each other.

The Ecumenical Center for Services to Evangelization and Popular Education (CESEP) based in São Paulo trains leaders in this approach. When it was founded in 1983, most of the participants were involved in different Roman Catholic pastoral commissions identified with liberation theology. Through the years its programs and methods changed. Today participants may be Catholic or Protestant. They may be leaders of CEBs or other social programs. Or they may be concerned with the ecumenical movement or feminist theology or Christian responsibility as citizens in a country adjusting from military rule to democracy. In an article Regina Soares Jukewicz describes how CESEP is meeting this challenge.

> We try to act in a democratic and transparent way between ourselves and with students. This is not always easy, and we have not always been successful. However, if we are unable to build democratic relationships in our daily lives, there is little sense in talking of a democratic society.

The Institute for Religious Studies

An old house in the Gloria section of Rio is the home of the Institute for Religious Studies (ISER). Its departments of liturgical renewal, women, youth, communications, blackness in Brazil, and other subjects bustle with activity. It is not only recognized by Roman Catholics and Protestants as a unique source of study and reflection but also by university centers, who use its library as a resource for religious matters. It was one of the first church-related programs to approach the subject of HIV and AIDS in a public forum.

When it set up a program of Women and Faith, its director did not know if the Catholics, Protestants, Jews, and followers of African religions who took part would be able to communicate with one another. The program was not only a success but led to a more serious study of blackness in Brazil — from a woman's experience. Several of its videos on life in the slums of Rio have been shown in the United States on public television. ISER fills a unique role in the ecumenical community as it provides a forum for people to meet and talk together on matters of faith in daily life.

KOINONIA: Ecumenical Presence and Service

KOINONIA is the main heir to an earlier ecumenical institution, the Evangelical Center for Information (CEI). In 1965, a year after the start the military dictatorship, CEI asked a question in its bulletin: "In various parts of the world, Christians protest against injustices and proclaim the will of God for the social order. What does our silence, the silence of Brazilian Protestantism, mean?" The positive response by both Protestant and Catholic readers was startling. Within a short time Catholics were participating in the center, making the "E" in the name stand for "Ecumenical."

In 1974 the center became CEDI with the addition of "Documentation" to its name. By 1983, CEDI was recognized for its publications; its consultant work for the Roman Catholic pastoral commissions, Protestant churches, and ecumenical bodies; its documentation of the situation of the indigenous peoples; its work in popular education; and its support of the peasant's and workers' movements. In 1992 it was the only organization in Brazil considered objective enough to become the coordinator of the Global Forum, the nongovernmental organizations' program, at the meeting of the United Nations conference on the environment in Rio. In 1994 CEDI officially ended its activities by dividing its programs into smaller autonomous units. KOINONIA: Ecumenical Presence and Service, inherited from CEDI the task of theological reflection with an emphasis on the struggles for human dignity and citizens' rights and solidarity. It continues the publication of theological material and work with the pastoral commissions.

Ecumenical Coordination of Services

Salvador is the base of the Ecumenical Coordination of Services (CESE). Organized by the Lutheran, Methodist, Episcopal, Brazil for Christ, United Presbyterian, and Roman Catholic churches, its primary purpose is to coordinate and provide services for churches in their programs with the poor and the oppressed. It trains church workers and leaders in popular movements. It is also a clearing house for new programs and a consulting body for the World Council of Churches and the National Council of Churches of Christ in the USA.

In 1989 CESE joined with the National Council of Christian Churches in Brazil in sponsoring a seminar on the national debt and the churches. It was a call to the churches to consider the economic situation of the country in the light of their faith. Knowing they could not solve the problem, the participants asked the churches to undertake serious study and formulate ethical guidelines to share with the government and private institutions. They also reminded the churches that Jesus came that people might have "abundant life." And they committed themselves to support the poor in their struggle for bread, dignity, and freedom as part of the mission of Jesus Christ.

The Group for Protestant Missionary Work

Although world attention has been drawn to the plight of the Indians in the Amazon rain forest, the churches have been concerned about the indigenous peoples across the entire nation. In August 1979 representatives of the Lutheran, Methodist, and Presbyterian churches met together in São Paulo with consultants from CEDI to develop a strategy for working with the indigenous people. A primary goal was to find ways for greater cooperation and integration in the work that denominations were already doing. Another was to create a network so that the missionaries would not be serving in isolation but would find ways to give each other support, a crucial matter during the difficult days of the military dictatorship.

In 1983 the network became a formal organization, the Group for Protestant Missionary Work (GTME), which was joined by the Anglican Church. The basic guidelines for the work were to help the Indians achieve self-determination, to join them in the defense of their land, to respect their culture, and to develop a pastoral ministry among them. Scilla Franco, first coordinator of GTME and later a Methodist bishop, lived and worked among the Kaiowas and the Terenas for several years. His writings about his experiences and discoveries continue to orient the work that GTME carries out today.

All the churches in Brazil today have their own unique mission and ministry whether they participate in ecumenical activities or not. As they strive to be faithful to the gospel, they share the good news in a variety of ways, bringing hope and a sense of identity to the people with whom they are in ministry. The words of a poor, black woman in the Northeast are indication of this work: "I may be poor. I may be black. I may be a woman. But the Church has taught me that God has daughters as well as sons. And I am one of God's daughters!"

Chapter 6

The North American Response

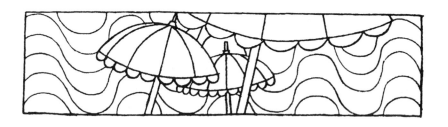

BLOW UPON US
A FRESH WIND

Pieces,
pieces,
a world in pieces, a life in pieces.

We want to live in a new era, O God,
we want to see signs of hope
telling us that it is possible
to bring the pieces together
and rebuild unity in our world.

We call on Your Spirit of Unity to come
from the four corners of the earth
and to blow new life in all beings.

Come, Spirit of God,
Blow upon us a fresh and renewing wind

that will fill us with courage and strength,
so that the pieces will become one body,
body of one world, body of one people.
Because this is how You created us;
this is how You want us to be.

— Ernesto Barros Cardoso,
translated by Joyce Hill

*A*S MEMBERS of the faith community that tries to be the faithful follower of Jesus Christ, we Christians in North America see ourselves faced by a challenging world situation. The global capitalist system excludes more and more people from full participation in the market and so from society in both the Northern and the Southern Hemisphere. Everywhere great wealth for a few is overbalanced by great misery for the many, especially in Brazil. How are Christians to respond?

Some Brazilian responses have been described in the preceding chapter. In this chapter we may consider two levels of response that are appropriate whether we live in North America or Brazil. The first is a change in the spirit of every believer. The second is a concrete process that local churches can enter.

Spiritual Change

As noted in chapter 5, some people in the Northern Hemisphere in the late twentieth century were beginning to change their views of society and the church. This change can be directed into three attitudes that will help us face the present challenge.

Humility

The first is an attitude of humility that is open to the action of the Spirit. The history of Christian communities is replete with examples of submission to the activities of the Spirit, which keeps open the possibilities of life for the sons and daughters of God. But we must discern where and how the Spirit is acting and with humbleness seek appropriate ways to respond.

As communities of the crucified and risen Lord, we must not allow ourselves to be crushed by the fear, deceit, and discouragement generated by our own suffering and that of the great majority of people, shoved aside as they are from the possibilities of life. On the contrary, we ought to resist. We ought to produce the fruits of the Spirit — love, joy, peace, patience, kindness, generosity, faithfulness, gentleness, self-control (Gal. 5:22–23). These fruits today constitute the wellspring of a counterculture that rejects the values of modernization, privatization, individualism, hedonism, and consumerism that characterize the systems of death in which we live. Only by such rejection shall we be able to be a sign of the coming reign of justice, peace, and dignity for all.

Creativity

The second attitude is to develop creativity, that is, to participate in creation rather than destruction in the world today. The gift of creativity comes from our being created in the image of God. As we read in the Bible, God gave us the responsibility to care for, preserve, and enjoy all creation. Therefore, the powers we use must be creative. In the New Testament the power of the Holy Spirit, like dynamite, is strong action, capable of opening, bursting through, the present scene. While the action is powerful, its primary intent is not to be a destructive action but a creative one, revealing new possibilities, new inspirations, and new hopes.

In the New Testament this creative power is an inseparable part of the spirituality of which Jesus tells us. If the task of Christians, in the North and South alike, is to be part of God's mission in the midst of creation, then we are called to build creatively, in every new time and historical situation, new missionary models, born out of our ability to discern together the action of the Spirit of God in our midst. This calling implies a permanent willingness to develop and stimulate the creative potential of our communities.

Rejection

The third attitude is to understand that rejection is a positive value in the gospel. Jesus emphasized in his ministry that salvation and the recovery of the integrity of Israel as the chosen people were now available to all. "The kingdom of God is among you" (Luke 17:21). This perspective removed him from the dominant religious life of Palestine at that time. Once he started his own community, Jesus found himself to be rejected and ostracized in the midst of his own people. This rejection was not only imposed on him by his adversaries, who represented the authority of the Temple and the Torah. It was consciously adopted by Jesus himself. In recovering and reinterpreting the prophetic tradition, Jesus completely rejected the formal religious requirements imposed by the Pharisees, the Sadducees, the Essenes, and the Zealots. Using the same symbols that had traditionally given the people meaning and direction, he offered a different interpretation of them, teaching that the true power and presence of God are not found in liturgical experience, sacred places, or bodies of doctrine but in people themselves, God's creatures.

Among God's creatures are those who count least in society. Certainly his proclamation of the reign of God was addressed to all. Not one was forgotten. All were invited. But just as certainly, he addressed primarily three classes of persons, precisely those oppressed and rejected by Jewish society — the poor, including women and children; the sick, handicapped, and infirm; and such outcasts as tax collectors, prostitutes, and recognized sinners.

In creating a community of equals among the rejected and superfluous, Jesus associated with them, taking on also their condition of exclusion and rejection. Thus as one who had willingly become excluded and rejected by the world because of his love for the disinherited, he made public their human situation. Breaking with bigotry, he reasserted mercy and love as the basis for genuine humanity. He practiced deeds of generosity and welcome. He lived "as if seeing the invisible" (Hebrews), sorrowful but always rejoicing, poor but possessing all things and with the absolute certainty that we have here no lasting city but seek the homeland to come. Since we, in both North and South, live in societies that affirm self-assurance and acceptance of the status quo (not rocking the boat), we are challenged to be humble, creative, and rejected as we live out our gospel calling and explore new ways of relating and being in mission together.

The São Paulo Process

An experiment in mutual understanding in mission, the São Paulo Process was developed within an ecumenical structure on an international level. It can be adapted by local churches in relationship to Brazil.

When they met in St. Louis in 1990, Rozilda from Brazil and Gladys from Detroit shared their problems, dreams, and faith with each other. Each of them held a factory job and earned the minimum wage. Each was struggling to raise a family on a meager income. Each of them longed for a secure future for herself and her children. Each of them found a community in her church which sustained her. Neither of them spoke much of the other's language, but that barrier did not deter them from knowing the other was a sister whose faith united them. They were part of the São Paulo Process.

The historical pattern of relationships between the churches based in the United States and Canada and their

foreign missions has been that of donor and recipient. Discussion of mutuality and ecumenical sharing of resources by
churches participating in the World Council of Churches had
not moved beyond theory. So it was that in September 1985
the Committee on the Caribbean and Latin America (CCLA)
of the National Council of Churches in the USA planned a
meeting with the leaders of ecumenical programs for which
they gave financial support. They asked these representatives
to work with them to find a way in which they could look at
their common problems and seek common solutions.

In May 1986, leaders of sixty-four projects in twenty-seven
different countries in Latin America and the Caribbean met
in São Paulo with members of CCLA and representatives of
the United Church of Canada and the Anglican Church of
Canada. Bible study based on the Lord's Prayer set the tone
of the meeting. Analysis of the social, political, and economic situation in the South set the stage for the "donors"
to listen to the concerns and dreams of the "recipients." One
of their dreams was to change the traditional relationships
with the churches in the North, moving beyond "giving" and
"receiving" to mutual respect and confidence, beyond being
"donors" and "recipients" to being equal members of the
one church. "Giving" was no longer to be measured purely
in financial terms, for the faith and prophecy that the South
can share with the North has no dollar value. The São Paulo
Process was on its way.

It has not been an easy process, for it has required time to
create a climate of honesty and openness. Program leaders in
the South have had to appreciate and trust one another in a
time of diminishing funds. Leaders of churches in the North
have had to learn to share information about resources available for mission. Moving from "donor" to "recipient" has
been difficult for the North. They have developed a few models, which can be replicated and expanded by other groups.
Many more can be created depending on needs.

The first of the models brought Rozilda and Gladys together in exchange visits between the South and the North.

Women from a variety of backgrounds and work compared their experiences and shared their faith. First women from the South visited women in the North; then women from the North visited women in Brazil. Children from the streets and in situations of violence shared their experiences of survival. Crees in northwestern Canada, Cherokees in the southeastern United States, and Tobas in northern Argentina found common ground. This was just the beginning.

The São Paulo meeting in 1986 made few specific recommendations. A meeting in Indianapolis in 1989 established a covenant between the South and the North to increase the understanding of the social, economic, cultural, political, and theological ties between the two hemispheres. The primary goal of the process was to develop a method for sharing power equally. A greater awareness of the context of both North and South was necessary to achieve this goal.

A third meeting, held in Honduras in 1992, made specific recommendations about educational opportunities. The following can be used in local churches.

• Establish and strengthen direct links between churches in Brazil and churches in the North.

• Promote understanding of Brazil by groups from churches in the North visiting church-related groups in Brazil. These visits should go beyond "church tourism" to develop first-hand awareness of the cultural, social, political, and economic conditions in which the Brazilians live. They can include travel-study seminars, work experience, and volunteer experience in different programs.

• Provide opportunities for persons from various cultural backgrounds and experiences to meet their counterparts in Brazil, such as leaders of indigenous peoples, community organizers, environmentalists, youth, women, health-care workers.

- Focus exchange visits on specific areas of cooperation, such as the environment, peaceful ways to end violence, or alternative educational opportunities for school dropouts.

- Provide opportunities to explore the rich cultural and religious heritage in Brazil. A list of readings and films is given in the back of this book.

- Use funds that would have provided a trip to Brazil to give brothers and sisters from Brazil the opportunity to visit local churches in the North. Some churches have programs that allow a person or family from another country to spend six months to a year as "missionary to the North."

A biblical and theological grounding is a crucial aspect of the São Paulo Process. As church people of the North develop relationships with the people of Brazil, those of the North will learn that faith is a crucial aspect of the graciousness of the Brazilians, strengthened perhaps by their living in a heartless system. In that learning the Northerners, aware of the injustices in their own society, may find their own faith deepened.

A group of laymen from Illinois learned this lesson as they visited the sprawling slum of Rocinha in Rio. From the front patio of the Methodist Church they could see the beautiful Copacabana beach far below in one direction. In the other, up above, they could see the back of the magnificent statue of Christ the Redeemer with outstretched arms blessing the city below. One of men asked the pastor, "How do these people feel when they look up and see that Christ has turned his back on them?"

The pastor was stunned by the question. He did not attempt to answer but called one of the church members over to join in the conversation. "This visitor has a question. 'How do you feel when you look up and see that Christ has turned his back on you?'" The church member, a simple man of faith, had an immediate answer.

"Christ has not turned his back on us! Hasn't this visitor read his Bible? Doesn't he know that after Jesus' resurrection the angel said that Jesus had gone ahead of the disciples to Galilee? Turned his back on us? No way! He is going ahead of us. He is our leader, and we are following him."

Appendix

Table 1
Foreign Corporations in Brazil in 1991

Company	Sector	Stockholders
1. Autolatina	Automotive	German, U.S.
2. Souza Cruz	Alcohol and tobacco	British
3. Shell	Oil	British
4. GMB	Automotive	U.S.
5. Esso	Oil	U.S.
6. Varig	Transportation	Brazilian
7. Mercedes-Benz	Automotive	German
8. Carrefour	Supermarkets	French
9. Nestlé	Foodstuffs	Swiss
10. IBM	Computers	U.S.
11. Texaco	Oil	U.S.
12. Atlantic	Oil	U.S.
13. Fiat	Automotive	Italian
14. Gessy Lever	Hygiene/sanitation	Dutch
15. C. R. Almeida	Heavy construction	Brazilian

SOURCE: *Exame,* August 1992, pp. 46–47; cited in *História do Brasil* by Boris Fausta (São Paulo: Fdusp, 1995), p. 542.

Table 2
Population and Income

The poorest 90% of the population received in
   1981, 53.4% of the national income
   1989, 46.8% of the national income
The richest 10% of the population received in
   1981, 46.6% of the national income
   1989, 53.2% of the national income
Notice that the figures are the same, only reversed in favor
of the wealthy.

The poorest 50% of the population received in
   1981, 13.4% of the national income
   1989, 10.4% of the national income
The richest 1% of the population received in
   1981, 13.0% of the national income
   1989, 17.3% of the national income
In 1981, the richest 1% earned as much as the poorest 50%.
In 1989, the richest earned 66% more than the poorest.

The poorest 10% of the population received in
   1981, 0.9% of the national income
   1989, 0.6% of the national income
In less than a decade, the poorest lost 32.3% of its original
participation in the gross national product.

SOURCE: Adapted from Paulo Schilling, *Brasil: A pior distribução de renda do planeta* (São Paulo: Cedi: Koinonia, 1994), 67.

Glossary

bandeirantes.	Small armed bands of adventurers.
caboclo.	Person of Indian and white ancestry.
candomblé.	African Brazilian religion.
capoeira.	African foot fighting that is now a street dance.
CCLA.	Committee on the Caribbean and Latin America, within the NCCC.
CEI.	Evangelical Center of Information. Became CEDI, became KOINONIA.
CENACORA.	Committee to Combat Racism.
CESE.	Ecumenical Coordination of Services.
CLAI.	Latin American Council of Churches.
CNBB.	National Conference of Brazilian Bishops (R.C.).
CONIC.	National Council of Christian Churches in Brazil (R.C. and Prot.).
egums.	In Bantu belief, wandering souls of ancestors.
empate.	Form of passive resistance.
favela.	Slum in Rio de Janeiro, and by extension elsewhere.
feijoada.	National dish of black beans, pork, rice, manioc flour, spices.

FUNABEM.   National Foundation for the Well-Being of the Minor.

FUNAI.   National Indian Foundation.

garimpeiros.   Goldminers.

Iemanjá.   In *candomblé,* Queen of the Waters, associated with the Virgin Mary.

macumba.   African Brazilian religion with elements of magic and Indian animism.

mestizo.   Person of mixed ancestry.

mulatto.   Person of African and white ancestry.

mineiros.   Natives of Minas Gerais.

NCCC.   National Council of the Churches of Christ in the USA

orixá.   African divinity.

paulistas.   Natives of São Paulo.

seringueiros.   Rubber tappers.

sertão.   Backlands in the Northeast, subject to drought.

SPI.   Service for the Protection of Indians.

terreiro.   *Candomblé* temple.

Selected Readings and Films

Books

Nonfiction

Adriance, Madeleine C. *Promised Land: Base Christian Communities and the Struggles for the Amazon.* Albany: State University of New York Press, 1995.

Archdiocese of São Paulo. *Torture in Brazil.* Translated by Jaime Wright. New York: Vintage Books, 1986.

Barbe, Dominique. *Grace and Power, Basic Communities and Non-Violence in Brazil.* Maryknoll, N.Y.: Orbis Books, 1987.

Bastide, Roger, *The African Religions in Brazil.* Baltimore: Johns Hopkins University Press, 1978.

Becker, Bertha K., and Claudio A. Egler. *Brazil: A New Regional Power in the World Economy.* Cambridge: Cambridge University Press, 1992.

Berryman, P. *Liberation Theology.* New York: Pantheon, 1987.

Boff, Clodovis. *Feet on the Ground Theology: A Brazilian Journey.* Maryknoll, N.Y.: Orbis Books, 1987.

Boff, Leonardo. *Liberation Theology from Confrontation to Dialogue.* Maryknoll, N.Y.: Orbis Books, 1986.

Boff, Leonardo, and Clodovis Boff. *Salvation and Liberation.* Maryknoll, N.Y.: Orbis Books, 1984.

Burns, E. Bradford. *A History of Brazil.* 3rd ed. New York: Columbia University Press, 1993.

Câmara, Dom Hélder. *The Desert Is Fertile.* Maryknoll, N.Y.: Orbis Books, 1974.

Cook, Guillermo. *The Expectation of the Poor: Latin American Based Ecclesial Communities in Protestant Perspective.* Maryknoll, N.Y.: Orbis Books, 1985.

Da Matta, Roberto. *Carnivals, Rogues, and Heroes: An Interpretation of the Brazilian Dilemma.* Notre Dame, Ind.: University of Notre Dame Press, 1993.

de Broucker, J. *Dom Hélder Câmara: The Violence of a Peacemaker.* Maryknoll, N.Y.: Orbis Books, 1970.

Degler, C. *Neither Black nor White: Slavery and Race Relations in Brazil and the United States.* New York: Macmillan, 1971.

94

de Jesus, Carolina Maria. *Child of the Dark*. New York: Dutton, 1962.

Dimenstein, Gilberto. *Brazil: War on Children*. New York: Monthly Review Press, 1992.

do Nascimento, A. *Brazil: Mixture or Massacre*. Translated by E. Nascimento. Dover, Mass.: Majority Press, 1989.

Finton, Heather. *Generous Living: The Joys and Heartaches of Ministry Overseas*. Toronto: Anglican Book Centre, 1997.

Freyre, G. *The Mansions and the Shanties: The Making of Modern Brazil*. Berkeley: University of California Press, 1986.

————. *The Masters and the Slaves: A Study in the Development of Brazilian Civilization*. Translated by S. Putman. Berkeley: University of California Press, 1964.

Galvin, Irene F. *Hard Lives, High Spirits*. Tarrytown, N.Y.: Marshall Cavendish Corp., 1996.

Gennino, Angela, ed. *Amazonia: Voices from the Rainforest*. San Francisco: Rainforest Action Network, 1990.

Gil-Montero, M. *Brazilian Bombshell: The Biography of Carmen Miranda*. New York: Donald I. Fine, 1989.

Guider, Margaret E. *Daughters of Rahab*. Minneapolis: Fortress, 1995.

Hess, David J. *Samba in the Night: Spiritism in Brazil*. New York: Columbia University Press, 1994.

Hewett, W. E. *Base Christian Communities and Social Change in Brazil*. Lincoln: University of Nebraska Press, 1991.

Krich, John. *Why Is This Country Dancing?* New York: Simon & Schuster, 1993.

Landes, Ruth. *City of Women*. Albuquerque: University of New Mexico Press, 1994.

Lernoux, Penny. *Cry of the People*. Garden City, N.Y.: Doubleday & Co., 1980.

Mainwaring, Scott. "Grassroots Catholic Groups and Politics in Brazil." In *The Progressive Church in Latin America*, edited by S. Mainwaring and A. Wilde. Notre Dame, Ind.: University of Notre Dame Press, 1989.

Martin, David. *Tongues of Fire: The Explosion of Protestantism in Latin America*. Oxford: Basil Blackwell, 1990.

Page, Joseph A. *The Brazilians*. Reading, Mass.: Addison-Wesley Publishing Co., 1995.

Patai, Daphne. *Brazilian Women Speak: Contemporary Life Stories*. New Brunswick, N.J.: Rutgers University Press, 1988.

Payne, L. *Brazilian Industrialists and Democratic Change*. Baltimore: Johns Hopkins University Press, 1994.

Ramos, Graciliano. *Barren Lives*. Translated by R. Dimmick. Austin: University of Texas Press, 1965.

Revkin, A. *The Burning Season: The Murder of Chico Mendes and the Fight for the Amazon Rain Forest*. Boston: Houghton-Mifflin Co., 1994.

Scheper-Hughes, Nancy. *Death Without Weeping: The Violence of Everyday Life in Brazil*. Berkeley: University of California Press, 1992.

Shoumatoff, Alex. *The World Is Burning: Murder in the Rain Forest*. New York: Avon, 1991.

96 Selected Readings and Films

Skidmore, Thomas E. *Black into White: Race and Nationality in Brazilian Thought.* New York: Oxford University Press, 1988.
———. *Fact and Myth: Discovering a Racial Problem in Brazil.* Notre Dame, Ind.: University of Notre Dame Press, 1992.
———. *The Politics of Military Rule in Brazil 1964–95.* New York: Oxford University Press, 1993.
Summ, G. Harvey, William H. Beezley, and Judith Ewell. *Brazilian Mosaic: Portraits of a Diverse People and Culture.* Wilmington, Del.: SR Books, 1995.
Taliani, Alberto. *Brazil.* New York: Smithmark Publishers, 1995. (Color photos and text.)

Fiction

Amado, Jorge. *Dona Flor and Her Two Husbands.* New York: Avon, 1977.
———. *Gabriella, Clove, and Cinnamon.* New York: Avon, 1988.
———. *The Golden Harvest.* New York, Avon, 1992.
———. *Violent Land.* New York: Avon Books, 1988.
———. *War of the Saints.* New York: Bantam Books, 1995.

For Children

Cousteau Society. *An Adventure in the Amazon.* New York: Simon & Schuster, 1992.
Lourie, Peter. *Amazon: A Young Reader's Look at the Last Frontier.* Honesdale, Pa.: Boyds Mill Press, 1991.
Mennonite Central Committee. *Brazil.* Latin America/Caribbean Series. Akron, Pa.: Mennonite Central Committee, 1997.
Schwartz, David M. *Yanomani: People of the Amazon.* Vanish People Series. New York: Lothrop, Lee & Shepard Books, 1993.
Waterlow, Julia. *The Amazon.* Rivers of the World Series. Chatham, N.J.: Raintree Steck-Vaughn Publishers, 1993.

Films

Black Orpheus. A French film about Carnival in Rio.
Hour of the Star. A young woman from the Northeast in a city.
The Mission. A Jesuit mission to the Guarani Indians in the eighteenth century.
Peixote: The story of a street child.
Vidas Secas: (Barren Lives) Northeast migrants in the city. With subtitles.

Videography

NOTE: All resources listed below are ½" VHS format unless otherwise noted.

Primary Resource

BRAZIL: A Faithful Response

Sale: $29.95   1996   26 min.
Rental: $15.00

Brazil is the fifth largest country in the world. It has many people of active faith, large cities, much poverty, and many issues confronting it. This resource video for the Education for Mission study on Brazil looks at issues of equality, the welfare of children, and spirituality in contemporary Brazil. It highlights the involvement of three Protestant denominations in the *favelas* of Rio de Janeiro, among street children, and in an exciting media ministry. Lutheran pastor Mozart Noronha looks at the line between rich and poor and drug use concerns in Ipanema. The Peoples' Central Institute, founded by Methodist missionaries, works with street children. Presbyterian pastor Caio Fabio takes his concern for social justice to the radio airwaves and becomes well known throughout Brazil. Throughout, the faithful response of the Brazilian people to the needs of their country becomes clear. Study guide included.

Available for *sale only* from
     Friendship Press Distribution Office
     P.O. Box 37844
     Cincinnati, OH 45222-0844
     (513) 948-8733

Available for *rental only* from
     EcuFILM
     810 Twelfth Avenue, South
     Nashville, TN 37203
     (800) 251-4091

Secondary Resources

Banking on Life and Debt
Sale: $14.95   1995   30 min.

The video looks at how policies of the World Bank and the International Monetary Fund affect three countries: Ghana, Brazil, and the Philippines. In the middle segment, on Brazil, we see people eating from garbage dumps while crops are sold to pay off the world's largest foreign debt. The IMF took more money out of Brazil than it gave loans to that country, thus re-shaping Brazil's economy. The video paints a stark picture with a "strong medicine" approach to economic issues affecting Brazil. Study guide included.

> Available for *sale only* from
> Maryknoll World Productions
> P.O. Box 308
> Maryknoll, NY 10545-0308
> (800) 227-8523

Bento
Rental: $15.00   1989   14 min.

Though older, this brief documentary offers a snapshot overview of Brazil; then it follows a young man who leaves a small town to go to the large city of São Paulo. There he stays in a *favela* and discovers the discrimination that black Brazilians suffer. He gets involved, joins a youth group, and struggles with organizing people in the *favela* — assisted by a Maryknoll lay missioner. Street groups are shown meeting for reflection and prayer, expressing their faith in God.

> Available for *rental only* from
> EcuFILM [see above]

Brazil: The Gospel and the Base Communities
Sale: $29.95 (Can.)   1995   28:30 min.
$24.95 (U.S.)

Brazil is a nation of enormous wealth and staggering poverty; cities burgeon with the *favelas* of the displaced. While there are many church initiatives which seek to address this situation, all too often churches have sided with the interests of the powerful rather than the plight of the poor. The Base Church Community (CEB) movement seeks to change this situation. Its conviction is that, when unleashed, the gospel can empower the dispossessed to challenge injustice and inequality.

This video visits several Base Christian Communities, both urban and rural, and invites the viewer into the lives of the people in these communities. [UCCan]

Available for *sale only* from
Berkeley Studio, United Church of Canada
Atten. Nancy Gallinger
3250 Bloor Street, West
Etobicoke, ON M8X 2X4 Canada
(416) 231-7680 ex. 4042

The Earth Summit: What Next?

Sale: $25.00   1993   28 min.
Rental: $18.00

In mid-1993 in Rio de Janeiro a very significant "Earth Summit" was held under the auspices of UN nongovernmental agencies (NGOs) to look at ways to save the planet from environmental and social catastrophe. How much progress has been made and how much further do we have to go? U.S. Vice-president Al Gore remarked, "The ecological crisis is a spiritual crisis," setting the tone for this documentary's look at the role of the churches in this movement and how environmental issues can be understood as spiritual concerns. It illustrates how the world community can work together on a specific issue.

Available for sale and rental from
EcuFILM [see above]

The Fruits of the Forest

Sale: $29.95 (Can.)   1994   29 min.
        $24.95 (U.S.)

This video takes a look at threats to the rain forest by mining and other interests that are destroying and exploiting the land. One company is ecologically sensitive and looks to break the cycle of destroying the environment. The video presents an alternative vision for farming in the forest and shows what people are trying to do for themselves.

Available for *sale only* from
Berkeley Studio, United Church of Canada [see above]

Padre Cicero

Rental: $12.50   37 min.

This is the story of a passionate campaign to lift a local Roman Catholic priest in Brazil from mortal clergy to sainthood. It shows the distinctive role that Roman Catholicism plays in the lives of believers as it combines mysticism, worship, and elements of several cultures.

Available for *rental only* from
EcuFILM [see above]

Why We Care: Children and Crisis
Sale: $29.95   1992   27 min.
Rental: $18.00

After a segment on Guatemala, this United Methodist video looks at the killing of street children in Brazil, children who are our present and future. It provides a helpful view of how to use dance, visual arts, theater, and puppets as part of a program in survival education to reach the street children of São Paulo. A United Methodist production.

Available for sale and rental from
    EcuFILM [see above]

Women on the Front
Rental: $12.50   1996   35 min.

In this grass-roots view of women talking for themselves we see three stories of women's struggles from different corners of Brazil: Community Associations from Jardim Uchoa (in the Northeast), from Rancho Fundo (in the Southeast), and Nova Iguaçu (a city on Greater Rio's periphery). These are women who speak out in poor urban neighborhoods, identifying themselves with their neighbors and with the places where they live, educate their children, and work to build a democratic way of life. The video was produced as a joint project with the United Nations Development Fund for Women. It draws attention to the economic, legal, and social struggles facing many women in Brazilian cities.

Available for *rental only* from
    EcuFILM [see above]

Young and On Their Own
Sale: $24.95 (Can.)   1995   17 min.
      $19.95 (U.S.)

An updated version of *Hope Is the Last Thing to Die,* this documentary looks at street children (especially boys) and the pressures they face in the *favelas* — they are young, innocent, and vulnerable. One in ten children in Brazil are abandoned. This video shows the work of Church World Service and United Methodist Church workers among these street children. It strikes a balance between despair and hope in relating to the economic issues that these street children lift up.

Available for *sale only* from
    Berkeley Studio, United Church of Canada [see above]